Green's 2024 Trader Tax Guide

By Robert A. Green, CPA

Written by Robert A. Green, CPA

Edited by Star Johnson, CPA

Produced by Molly Flynn Goad

ISBN: 979-8-9895811-0-8

In publishing this guide, we made every effort to offer the most current, correct, and clearly expressed information possible. Nonetheless, inadvertent errors can occur, and tax laws and regulations governing personal finance and investing can change. The advice and strategies herein may not suit your unique tax situation. It's important to note that there is a risk of loss trading options, stocks, commodity futures, and foreign exchange products. Neither the publisher nor the author shall be liable for any loss of profit or any other commercial damages, including but not limited to special, incidental, consequential, or other damages that are incurred as a consequence of the use and application, directly or indirectly, of any information presented in this guide. If legal, tax advice, or other expert assistance is required, consider the services of a professional. We intended this guide for educational use only.

Excerpts from this guide also appear on the author's website, Greentradertax.com; Forbes.com; and third-party websites that feature content from Robert A. Green.

About Green & Company

Green & Company, Inc. (GreenTraderTax.com), the publisher of this guide, offers extensive educational resources for traders on its website, including a blog covering the latest topics, Webinars and recordings, and more. For more information, visit www.greentradertax.com.

Our motto: Be intelligent, creative, forward-thinking, cutting edge, and aggressive, but keep it legal. You deserve excellence in content, ideas, judgment, and decision-making. Thanks for being our customer and reading our guide.

Thank you to my colleagues at Green, Neuschwander & Manning for their help crafting our trader tax strategies. Special thanks to managing member Darren Neuschwander, CPA, and my co-editor, Star Johnson, CPA.

Sincerely,

Robert A. Green, CPA,
CEO of Green & Company, Inc.
GreenTraderTax.com

Table of Contents

Highlights

You can use *Green's 2024 Trader Tax Guide* to receive the tax breaks you're entitled to on your 2023 tax returns and execute tax strategies and elections for tax year 2024. Our guide covers the impact of recent tax laws on traders.

BUSINESS TRADERS FARE BETTER

Investors have restricted investment interest expense deductions. The Tax Cuts & Jobs Act (TCJA) suspended investment fees and expenses for 2018 through 2025. Investors have a capital-loss limitation against ordinary income ($3,000 per year) and wash-sale (WS) loss adjustments, which can trigger capital gains taxes on phantom income. Investors benefit from lower long-term capital gains rates on positions held for 12 months or more before a sale (0%, 15%, and 20%). If traders have long-term investment positions, this is also available to them.

Traders eligible for trader tax status (TTS) are entitled to many tax advantages. A sole proprietor (individual) TTS trader deducts business expenses, startup costs, margin interest, and home office expenses. TTS allows them to elect Section 475 MTM ordinary gain or loss treatment. To deduct health insurance and retirement plan contributions, a TTS trader needs an S-Corporation to create earned income with officer compensation. TTS traders use a pass-through entity (partnership or S-Corp) to arrange a state and local tax (SALT) cap workaround in many states.

TTS is different from the election of Section 475 MTM accounting. TTS is like an undergraduate university, and Section 475 is like graduate school. The 475 election converts new capital gains and losses into ordinary gains and losses, avoiding the $3,000 capital loss limitation. Only those qualifying to claim trader tax status may use Section 475 MTM accounting; investors may not. Section 475 trades are also exempt from wash sale loss adjustments. The 20% deduction on qualified business income (QBI) includes Section 475 ordinary income but excludes capital gains, interest, and dividend income.

A business trader can assess and claim trading-related business expenses after year-end and even go back three open tax years (by filing an amended tax return). TTS does not require an election. However, TTS traders (individuals or new taxpayer "entities" qualifying for TTS) may only use Section 475 MTM if they made an election appropriately. For more on TTS, see Chapter 1; for Section 475 election and deadlines, see Chapter 2.

CAN TRADERS DEDUCT TRADING LOSSES?

Deducting trading losses depends on the instrument traded, the trader's tax status, and various elections.

Many traders bought this guide, hoping to find a way to deduct their trading losses. Maybe they qualify for TTS, but that only gives them the right to take trading business expenses on Form 1040/Schedule C.

Securities, Section 1256 contracts, ETNs, and cryptocurrency trading receive default capital gain/loss treatment. Suppose a TTS trader did not file a Section 475 election on securities and commodities on time (i.e., by April 18, 2023 for 2023) or have Section 475 from a prior year. They are stuck with capital loss treatment on securities and Section 1256 contracts for 2023. Section 475 does not apply to ETN prepaid forward contracts (not securities) or cryptocurrencies (intangible property).

Capital losses offset capital gains without limitation, whether short-term or long-term, but a net capital loss on Schedule D is limited to $3,000 per year against other income. Excess capital losses carry over to the subsequent tax year(s).

Once taxpayers get in the capital loss carryover trap, they often face a problem: how to use up the capital loss carryover in the following year(s). If a taxpayer elects Section 475 by April 15, 2024 for 2024, the 2024 TTS trading gains will be ordinary rather than capital, thereby not utilizing the capital loss carryover from 2023. Once a trader has a capital loss carryover hole, they need a capital gains ladder to climb out of it and a Section 475 election to prevent digging an even bigger one. The IRS allows revocation of Section 475 elections if a Section 475 trader later decides they want capital gain/loss treatment again. Chapter 2 covers this topic in depth.

Traders with capital losses from Section 1256 contracts (such as futures) might be lucky if they had gains in Section 1256 contracts in the prior three tax years. On the top of Form 6781, traders can file a Section 1256 loss carryback election. This election allows taxpayers to offset their current-year net 1256 losses against prior-year net 1256 gains to receive a refund of taxes paid in prior years. TTS traders may elect Section 475 MTM on commodities, including Section 1256 contracts. Still, most elect it on securities only to retain the lower 60/40 capital gains tax rates on Section 1256 gains, where 60% is considered a long-term capital gain, even on day trades. The other 40% fall under ordinary income rates.

Taxpayers with losses trading forex contracts in the off-exchange Interbank market may be lucky. Section 988 for forex transactions receives ordinary gain or loss treatment by default, which means the capital-loss limitation doesn't apply. However, the forex loss isn't considered a business loss without TTS. Failing to qualify for TTS means you cannot include forex losses in your net operating loss (NOL) carryforward calculation, potentially making the forex loss a wasted loss since it also can't be added to the capital-loss carryover. If the taxpayer has another source of taxable income, the ordinary loss offsets it; the concern is when there is negative taxable income.

A TTS trader using Section 475 on securities has ordinary loss treatment, which avoids wash-sale loss adjustments and the $3,000 capital loss limitation. Section 475 ordinary losses offset income of any kind. However, Section 475 losses and TTS business expenses are subject to the excess business loss (EBL) limitation for tax years 2023 and 2024. Anything over the EBL threshold is a net operating loss (NOL) carryforward.

Those not using Section 475 must deal with wash-sale loss adjustments.

WASH-SALE LOSSES

Day and swing traders inevitably trigger WS loss adjustments amounting to tens or hundreds of thousands of dollars. You create a WS loss when you take a loss on a security and repurchase it within 30 days (after or before).

A wash sale reduces the cost basis on the position sold and adds the WS loss to the replacement position's cost basis, creating phantom taxable income and capital gains taxes.

It's okay to incur WS losses during the year, but avoid delaying them to the following year. Deferring a loss from November to December is acceptable; however, postponing a loss from December 2023 to January 2024 is not.

You should aim to "break the WS chain" at year-end. For example, sell your entire position in security A by Dec. 20, 2023, and don't repurchase it for 30 days — around Jan. 21, 2024. Waiting allows you to deduct the whole year of WS losses in 2023. See more about WS in Chapter 4.

EXCESS BUSINESS LOSS LIMITATION

In 2018, TCJA introduced an excess business loss (EBL) limitation. TCJA also repealed NOL carrybacks (except for farmers) and limited NOL carryforwards to 80% of the subsequent year's taxable income. Add EBL over the threshold to the NOL carryforward.

The 2020 CARES Act suspended TCJA's EBL and NOL changes for 2018, 2019, and 2020 and allowed five-year NOL carrybacks (i.e., a 2020 NOL carryback to 2015). TCJA's EBL and NOL carryforward rules apply for tax years 2021 through 2028.

See more about EBL and its thresholds in Chapter 2.

TAX TREATMENT ON FINANCIAL PRODUCTS

There are complexities in sorting through different tax treatment rules and tax rates. It often takes work to tell what falls into each category. To help our readers with this, we cover the many trading instruments and their tax treatment in Chapter 3. Here's a brief breakdown.

Securities have realized gain and loss treatment and are subject to WS rules and the $3,000 per year capital loss limitation on individual tax returns. Realization means income or loss when sold instead of mark-to-market (MTM) accounting. A Section 475 MTM election on securities avoids this issue.

Section 1256 contracts — including regulated futures contracts on U.S. commodities exchanges — are marked to market by default, so there are no wash-sale adjustments, and they receive lower 60/40 capital gains tax rates. Most TTS traders skip a Section 475 election on commodities to retain lower 60/40 capital gains rates.

Options have a wide range of tax treatments. An option is a derivative of an underlying financial instrument, and the tax treatment is generally the same. Equity options are taxed the same as equities, which are securities. Index options are derivatives of indexes, and broad-based indexes (stock index futures) are Section 1256 contracts. Simple and complex equity option trades have special tax rules on holding periods, adjustments, and more.

Forex receives ordinary gain or loss treatment on realized trades (including rollovers) unless a trader makes a contemporaneous capital gains election. In some cases, lower 60/40 capital gains tax rates on majors may apply under Section 1256(g).

Physical precious metals are collectibles; if a trader holds these capital assets for over one year, sales are subject to the collectibles' capital gains rate capped at 28%.

Cryptocurrencies are intangible property taxed like securities on Form 8949, but wash-sale loss and Section 475 rules do not apply because they are not securities.

Foreign futures are taxed like securities unless the IRS issues a revenue ruling allowing Section 1256 tax benefits.

ENTITIES FOR TRADERS

Entities can solidify TTS, unlock health insurance and retirement plan deductions, gain flexibility with a Section 475 election or revocation, prevent wash-sale losses with individual and IRA accounts, enhance a QBI deduction on Section 475 income less trading expenses, and provide a

SALT cap workaround. An entity return consolidates trading activity on a pass-through tax return, making life easier for traders, accountants, and the IRS. Trading in an entity allows separation from individual investments.

An LLC with an S-Corp election is generally the best choice for a single or married couple seeking health insurance and retirement plan deductions.

A spousal-member LLC taxed as a partnership can segregate business trading from investments to perfect use of TTS and Section 475 and provide a SALT cap workaround, turning non-deductible state and local taxes as itemized deductions into tax-deductible business expenses. See Chapter 7.

RETIREMENT PLANS FOR TRADERS

TTS S-Corps can unlock a retirement plan deduction by paying sufficient officer compensation in December 2023 when results for the year are evident.

Consider a Solo 401(k) retirement plan with an elective deferral amount up to a maximum of $22,500 (or $30,000 if age 50 or older with the $7,500 catch-up provision). The Solo 401(k) also has a profit-sharing plan (PSP) up to a maximum of $43,500.

The IRS raised the 401(k) elective deferral for 2024 to $23,000; the catch-up contribution remains at $7,500. See Chapter 8.

DEDUCTION ON QUALIFIED BUSINESS INCOME

In 2018, TCJA introduced a new tax deduction for pass-through businesses, including sole proprietors, partnerships, and S-Corps. Subject to haircuts and limitations, a pass-through business could be eligible for a 20% deduction on qualified business income (QBI).

Because TTS traders are considered a "specified service trade or business" (SSTB), taxable income above the following thresholds is not deductible: $364,200/$182,100 (married/other taxpayers) for 2023 and $383,900/$191,950 (married/other taxpayers) for 2024.

There is also a phase-out range above the threshold of $100,000/$50,000 (married/other taxpayers). The W-2 wage and property basis limitations apply within the phase-out range. TTS traders with an S-Corp usually have wages, whereas sole proprietor traders do not.

QBI for traders includes Section 475 ordinary income and loss and trading business expenses. QBI excludes capital gains and losses, Section 988 forex income or loss, dividends, and interest income.

For more information, see Chapter 7 and Chapter 17.

SALT CAP WORKAROUND

TCJA capped state and local income, sales, and property taxes (SALT) at $10,000 per year ($5,000 for married filing separately) and did not index it for inflation. About 30 states enacted SALT cap workaround laws.

Generally, elect to make a pass-through entity (PTE) payment on a partnership or S-Corp tax return filed by a business. It doesn't work with a sole proprietorship filing a Schedule C. PTE tax paid is a business expense deduction shown on the state K-1 like a withholding credit. Most states credit the individual's state income tax liability with the PTE payment amount. Essentially, this converts a non-deductible SALT itemized deduction (over the cap) into a business expense deduction from gross income.

DESK REFERENCE

Some readers use our guide as a desk reference to quickly find answers to specific questions. Others read this guide in its entirety. To accommodate desk-reference readers, we edit each chapter to stand alone, which inevitably means some chapters contain information covered in others.

Chapter 1

Trader Tax Status

Trader tax status (TTS) constitutes business expense treatment and unlocks meaningful tax benefits for those who qualify. The first step is to determine eligibility. If you qualify for TTS, you can claim some tax breaks, make tax elections, and take action to set up other tax advantages — like Section 475 MTM and employee-benefit plans — on a timely basis.

THERE'S NO ELECTION FOR TTS

Trader tax status is an optional tax status based on facts and circumstances. You do not need to make an election. You may qualify for TTS one year but not the next, so you should assess your eligibility yearly.

Those with TTS should consider a Section 475 election for ordinary gain or loss treatment to navigate around wash-sale loss adjustments and the $3,000 capital loss limitation. You might qualify for a 20% qualified business income (QBI) deduction on Section 475 trading gains. You must elect Section 475 on time; otherwise, you miss that boat until the next tax year.

PART-YEAR TTS EXAMPLE

Trader tax status qualification can be for part of a year. Perhaps a taxpayer qualified for TTS to start 2023 and quit or suspended active trading on June 30, 2023. This trader can include the partial-year qualification period on Schedule C or the pass-through entity tax return and deduct business expenses relating to the active trading period.

If elected, this trader may use Section 475 for trades made during the TTS period. However, starting July 1, 2023, the trader suspends TTS and Section 475 until they qualify for trader status in a subsequent tax year.

BUSINESS EXPENSE TREATMENT

Qualifying for TTS means a trader can use business treatment for trading expenses.

Business expenses include home office, education, Section 195 startup expenses, Section 248 organization expenses, margin interest, tangible property expense, Section 179 (100%) or 100% bonus depreciation, amortization on software, self-created automated trading systems (Section 174), seminars, market data, stock borrow fees, and much more. If TTS business expenses and home office deductions are $20,000, and the taxpayer's federal and state tax bracket is 40%, income tax savings is about $8,000.

The 2017 Tax Cuts & Jobs Act (TCJA) suspended "certain miscellaneous itemized deductions subject to the 2% floor," including investment fees and expenses, beginning in 2018. TCJA incentivizes traders to qualify for TTS.

TTS is allowed for the tax year ended and the prior three tax years with amended returns by including a Schedule C as a sole proprietor on individual accounts. (Note: Filing amended tax returns may increase the odds of IRS questions or exams, so before choosing this route, taxpayers should be sure they qualify for TTS.)

Full-time active traders generally qualify for TTS. Part-time traders can also be eligible, but doing so is more challenging. The bar is raised in the eyes of the IRS — especially if the trader has significant trading losses with business ordinary-loss treatment (Section 475) rather than capital-loss limitations. For more information about business expenses for TTS traders, see Chapter 5.

HOW TO QUALIFY

It's not easy to qualify for TTS. Currently, there's no statutory law with objective tests for eligibility. Subjective case law applies. Leading tax publishers have interpreted case law to show a two-part test to qualify for TTS:

1. "Taxpayer's trading activity must be substantial, regular, frequent, and continuous.
2. Taxpayer must seek to catch swings in daily market movements and profit from these short-term changes rather than profiting from long-term holding of investments."

IRS agents often refer to Chapter 4 in IRS Publication 550, "Special Rules for Traders." Here's an excerpt:

"The following facts and circumstances should be considered in determining if your activity is a securities trading business.

- Typical holding periods for securities bought and sold.
- The frequency and dollar amount of your trades during the year.
- The extent to which you pursue the activity to produce income for a livelihood.
- The amount of time you devote to the activity."

"Substantial, regular, frequent, and continuous" are subjective. Furthermore, case law doesn't give a bright-line test with numbers, except for the holding period. Recent tax court cases have set a further precedent (see Chapter 11).

The IRS publication mentions the holding period, frequency, dollar amount of trades, and the time devoted by the taxpayer. It also says the intention to make a livelihood is vital in defeating the hobby-loss rules. Trading is not personal or recreational, which are the key terms in hobby-loss case law.

GOLDEN RULES

We base our golden rules on trader tax court cases, our experience with IRS, and state controversy for traders. Volume, frequency, and average holding period are the "big three" because they are more accessible for the IRS to verify.

Volume: The 2015 tax court case Poppe vs. Commissioner is a helpful reference. Poppe made 720 total trades per year/60 per month. We recommend an average of four transactions per day, four days per week, 16 trades per week, 60 trades a month, and 720 per year. Count each open and closing transaction separately.

Here's an example. Let's figure you're available to trade 230 days per year. (This accounts for personal days and holidays taken during the approximately 250 days the securities markets are open each year.) A 75% frequency of 230 days equals 173 days per year, so 720 total trades divided by 173 trading days equals about four daily transactions. (Some traders scale in and out of trades; count each separately.)

Options traders have multi-legged positions on complex options trades. Our position is that you may count each trade confirmation of a complex options trade if you enter the legs separately, although the tax court has not addressed that issue yet. Most traders enter a complex options trade as one order, and the broker breaks down the legs, so you should not count the legs separately.

If you initiate a trade order and the broker breaks down the lot sizes without your involvement, it's wise not to count the extra trade volume.

Unlike securities trades, forex and futures aren't listed line by line on tax returns, so the IRS can't see the volume of trading in tax form details. It's wise to provide a detailed description of trading volume in tax return footnotes.

In the 2013 Endicott and Nelson tax court cases, the IRS further delineated between "substance" and "volume." Substance refers to the size of trades and materiality, whereas volume is the number of transactions during the year. See Chapter 11 for further information about the case on this point. Cryptocurrency traders may appear to have thousands of trades, but they have far fewer. Many crypto exchanges break down one trade order into tens or hundreds of trade executions. Cryptocurrency traders should count orders — not the multiple executions they did not initiate.

Trade executions count, not unexecuted trades.

Closing option trades count, yet option assignments/expirations do not.

Frequency: Execute trades on close to four of five days per week, around a 75% frequency rate. Securities trades may use a five-day week for the denominator, but futures may use six days if the individual trades Sunday night. If you enter or exit a trading business during the year, you must maintain the frequency rate during the TTS period. Time off from the execution of trades should be for a reasonable number of vacation and personal days. TTS is a job where the markets are your boss.

The IRS denied TTS to equity options traders in the Holsinger, Assaderaghi, Endicott, and Nelson court cases. They only traded two to three days per week; hence, I suggest executing trades on close to four days per week for a securities trader. Four divided by the five days securities markets are open gives an 80% trading frequency rate. (See Chapter 11.)

Holding period: The IRS stated that the average holding period is the most crucial TTS factor. In the Endicott court, the IRS said the average holding period must be 31 days or less. That's a bright-line test. If your average holding period is more than 31 days, you won't qualify for TTS despite all your other factors.

It's more natural for day and swing traders to meet the holding period requirement. Taxpayers must only count TTS positions; segregated investment and retirement accounts aren't allowed.

Monthly options traders face challenges in holding periods. They may have average holding periods of over one month if they trade monthly and longer expirations. Holsinger was a monthly options trader with average holding periods of one to two months. Holsinger's case is from 2008; nowadays, TTS traders focus on trading weekly options expirations, many of which are eligible for TTS.

If an equities and equity options trader holds 80% of his trades for one day and the other 20% for 35 days, then the average holding period is well under 31 days. Whether the IRS might apply weighted averages to the average holding period is unclear.

Many traders commence trading in an investment account holding significant long-term equity positions that they trade options around to enhance income. The IRS might calculate the holding period based on long-term equity positions and options trading, which likely undermines TTS. That happened in many of the tax court cases discussed above. Traders need to segregate trading positions from investments on the individual level and consider a TTS entity for ring-fencing trades if there is an overlap between trading and investments.

Trades full-time or part-time: Part-time and money-losing traders face more IRS scrutiny, and individuals face more challenges than entity traders.

Full-time options traders actively trading significant portfolios may not qualify because they don't have enough volume and frequency, and their average holding period is over 31 days. On the other hand, a part-time trader with a full-time job may qualify as a day and swing trader in securities, meeting all our golden rules.

Hours: Spends more than four hours per day, almost every market day, working on the trading business. All-time counts include the execution of trade orders, research, administration, accounting, education, travel, meetings, and more. Most active business traders spend more than 40 hours per week in their trading business. Part-time traders usually have more than four hours per day. In one tax exam our firm handled, the IRS agent brought up material participation rules (Section 469), which require 500 hours of work per year (generally). Most business traders easily surpass 500 hours. However, Section 469 doesn't apply to trading businesses under its "trading rule" exemption. Without this exemption, taxpayers could generate passive-activity income by investing in hedge funds, and the IRS did not want that.

Avoid sporadic lapses. The IRS has successfully denied TTS in a few court cases by arguing that the trader had too many intermittent lapses in trading, such as taking several months off during the year. Traders can take vacations, sick time, and personal time off like everyone else. Some traders take a break from active trading to recover from recent losses and learn new trading methods and markets. Explain gaps to the IRS in tax-return footnotes. Retooling and education during a lapse in trade executions still may count for the continuous business activity (CBA) standard. However, the IRS currently does not give credence to CBA for TTS. We recommend traders keep proper records of their time spent as support.

The IRS doesn't respect new traders who enter and exit it too quickly, primarily if that trader seeks a large IRS refund by deducting a Section 475 MTM ordinary loss on an individual tax return.

Some traders must temporarily stop for several months for health reasons. It's unclear if the IRS will respect that as a valid interruption of a trading business activity.

Intention: Traders intend to run a business and make a living, but it doesn't have to be their exclusive or primary means of making a living. The key word is "a" living, which means it can be a supplemental living.

Many traders enter an active trading business while still working a full-time job. Technology advancements, flexible job schedules, and remote work make it possible to carry on both activities simultaneously.

It's not a good idea to try to achieve TTS within a business entity already principally conducting a different type of business activity. It's better to form a new trading entity. Trading an existing business's available working capital seems like a treasury function and sideline, which can deny trader tax breaks if the IRS looks. It's also confusing for QBI and other tax issues.

Filing as a sole proprietor on a Schedule C is allowed and used by many, but it's not the best tax filing strategy for a part-time trader. An individual tax return shows a taxpayer's job and other business activities or retirement, which may undermine TTS in the eyes of the IRS. The IRS tends to think trading is a secondary activity and may seek to deny TTS. It's best to form a separate entity dedicated to trading only.

Consider a trading entity when income tax savings outweigh the entity costs, including tax compliance services, payroll service, payroll taxes with TTS S-Corps, and other entity costs like minimum or franchise taxes. (Chapter 7 covers entities.)

Several years ago, we spoke with one IRS agent who argued that the trader did not make a living since he had perennial trading losses. That's okay because the rule refers to intention, not the actual results. The hobby-loss limitations don't apply to TTS traders because trading is not recreational or personal.

Operations: Has significant business equipment, education, business services, and a home office. Most business traders have multiple monitors, computers, mobile devices, trading services, subscriptions, education expenses, high-speed broadband, wireless, and a home office. Some have staff. The IRS needs to see a meaningful trading business operation. How can one run a business without a dedicated space? Casual investors rarely have as elaborate an office setup as TTS traders. Suppose a trader uses a home office space exclusively for business rather than personal use. The tax return should reflect this because it is not only a valid home office deduction, but it also supports the fact that there is legitimate business activity. The home office deduction is no longer a red flag with the IRS and is not a complicated calculation. (See home office deductions in Chapter 5.) Some TTS traders use just a laptop, and that's okay.

Account size: Has a material account size. Securities traders need to have $25,000 on deposit with a U.S.-based broker to achieve pattern day trader (PDT) status. With PDT, they can day trade using up to a 4:1 margin rather than 2:1. Otherwise, they can't day trade and will have difficulty qualifying for TTS. The $25,000 amount seems substantial enough to impress the IRS.

Many new traders don't want to risk $25,000 trading securities; they prefer to trade futures or forex, all allowing mini-account sizes of $5,000 or less. However, a small $5,000 account size won't impress the IRS — more capital equates to a better chance for qualification. We would like to see more than $15,000.

Adequate account size depends on one's overall net worth and cash flow. Millionaires may need larger account sizes, whereas some unemployed traders without much cash flow or young traders may get by with smaller accounts. A trader may also be able to factor in capital invested in equipment and startup costs.

Trading and investing in one account can undermine TTS. Traders often combine trading with long-term investing in one brokerage account. Traders use portfolio margining to borrow funds on long-term investments to trade options around those positions for enhancing income. For example, a trader might invest in Apple equity and trade Apple equity options around those investment positions to manage risk. The other reason is to avoid trading naked options, which requires holding the underlying equity.

The IRS can view this account as part of investment activity, and the holding period on investments often drags the average holding period above the 31-day requirement. The IRS might apply a weighted average with investment positions outweighing the size of trading positions.

To qualify for TTS, consider a separate brokerage account for trading vs. investing. But that will restrict portfolio margining as brokers do not allow it across multiple accounts.

If you invest in big tech and trade options on the same symbols, consider further segregation: A trading entity with TTS and Section 475, so the IRS cannot apply 475 MTM to your investments.

One individual account might be okay if you invest in ETFs, trade equities, and equity options. It can work because there is no overlap in symbols. Be careful to identify your investments on a contemporaneous basis.

WHAT DOESN'T QUALIFY?

Automated trading, using a trade copying service or software, engaging a professional outside investment manager, and trading in retirement funds do not qualify for TTS.

1. Outside-developed automated trading systems. These programs are becoming more popular. An entirely canned ATS with little to no involvement by the trader doesn't qualify for TTS. The IRS may view an outside-developed ATS the same as a trader who uses a broker to make most buy/sell decisions and executions.

However, if the trader can show they are very involved with designing and building the ATS, the IRS may count the ATS-generated trades in the TTS analysis. That includes but is not limited to writing the code or algorithms and setting the entry and exit signals. Many ATS traders use API scripting for automated execution with their brokerage platform. Self-creation of the ATS needs to be significant to count for TTS. Making a few choices in an outside-developed ATS building block service won't cut it.

Some traders don't have programming experience, but they have financial and trading experience. They design the ATS and hire an outside programmer to translate their specifications into a computer language.

It's helpful if these traders show they spend more than four hours daily working in the trading business, including time for ATS maintenance, back-testing, and modifications. I have not yet seen the IRS challenge ATS in exams or court cases, but I feel it may react this way when it comes up.

If traders spend much money on an outside-developed ATS that doesn't qualify as part of their trading business, then TCJA suspends those investment expenses. Traders need to realize that the IRS may connect the dots and realize they are using an ATS. A full-scale exam can uncover these facts. Consider the analogy of an airplane pilot using manual and automated systems. A trader needs to be a pilot in the cockpit, not in the cabin as a passenger.

2. Trade copying service. Some traders use trade copying software or service (TCS). Trade copying is like a canned ATS or outside adviser, where the copycat trader might not qualify for TTS on those trades. For example, a trade coaching and education company offers a TCS that suggests several daily transactions with exact entry and exit points and stop-loss orders. The trader decides which trades to make and executes them manually.

If the trader follows the TCS tightly and does not significantly depart from its suggestions, an IRS agent might deny TTS. On the other hand, if the trader cherry-picks a minor percentage of the suggested trades, sets different stop-loss orders, and waits longer on entry and exit executions, they might qualify for TTS. The TCS vendor might state they are not providing investment management services, but that doesn't mean their customer achieves TTS using the TCS.

3. Engaging a money manager. Hiring a registered investment adviser (RIA) or commodity trading adviser (CTA) — whether duly registered or exempt from registration — to trade one's account doesn't count toward TTS qualification. However, hiring an employee or independent contractor to help trade their funds should qualify, providing the taxpayer is a competent trader. Decades-old tax court cases show that using outside brokers and investment advisers to make trading decisions undermines TTS.

When a taxpayer sets up a small LLC, there are nuances between engaging an independent outside manager vs. a supervised inside trader. If the engaged trader is a registered investment adviser, they are clearly in the business of being an external manager, and TTS is impossible. But if the trader only trades inside the taxpayer's LLC under the taxpayer's direction, it may be possible to achieve TTS.

Proprietary trading firms engage independent contractors or LLC-member proprietary traders to trade the firm's capital. In this situation, the prop firm achieves TTS. Prop traders are not using their funds, although they may have a retail trading account. In most cases, non-employee prop traders can deduct their business expenses on their tax return Schedule C for independent contractors and Schedule E for LLC K-1 members. (See Chapter 12 on proprietary trading.)

With married couples, if spouse A has an individual brokerage account in their name only and gives power of attorney to spouse B, the IRS won't grant TTS even if spouse B meets all the golden rules for TTS. The IRS doesn't consider spouse B an owner of the account. In this case, the IRS treats spouse A as an investor and spouse B as an investment manager. Married couples can solve this problem using a joint individual account or trading in a spousal-owned entity. It's best to list the trading spouse first on the account.

4. Trading retirement funds. Trading in non-taxable retirement accounts doesn't contribute to TTS qualification. Actively trading in retirement plans offers an opportunity to build tax-free compounded returns, particularly for individuals ineligible for TTS in taxable accounts. Caution: Trading substantially identical positions between an individual taxable account and IRA account can trigger a permanent wash-sale loss in a taxable account that doesn't move into the IRA. See Chapter 4.

FALLING SHORT

If the trading activity falls short of the conditions in trader tax court cases, the IRS may scrutinize a return and challenge TTS. The IRS may examine a return anyway, but if taxpayers meet our golden rules, they have an excellent chance at TTS. Anytime there is uncertainty surrounding qualification, we recommend consulting a trader tax expert to review the facts and circumstances to ensure a solid position for claiming TTS.

Filing an entity tax return is safer than filing a Schedule C as a sole proprietor because an entity attracts less IRS attention. If a taxpayer trades in an entity, the same golden rule standards apply for TTS qualification — otherwise, it's an investment company like most hedge funds. On an entity return, trading income and losses are displayed alongside business expenses, making a profitable trading business look promising, which could warrant less attention. Conversely, on an individual return, Schedule C traders look like a losing business since a trader reports trading gains on other tax forms like Form 8949 for securities, Form 6781 for futures, and Form 4797 for Section 475 MTM trades. The IRS often does not connect Schedule C expenses and those other tax forms with TTS-related trading gains and losses. Using different tax forms is a structural problem for sole proprietor traders. Chapter 6 provides some solutions.

Part-time traders with full-time jobs should consider a separate entity tax return to claim TTS safely. A stand-alone trading business looks better on the entity than individual tax returns. However, it might not be worth the extra entity costs to appear better in the eyes of the IRS.

ADD SCHEDULE C

Taxpayers who qualified for TTS in 2023 and have trading business expenses, startup costs, and home office expenses can add a Schedule C to their 2023 tax return. Even though the Section 475 deadline has passed (April 18, 2023) and an ordinary business deduction for trading capital losses is not permitted, TTS allows a trading expenses deduction, which could generate significant tax savings.

Some business traders feel satisfied with operating as sole proprietors (with a Schedule C) because it appears less complicated than using a separately filed entity return. They can claim TTS after year-end, which often costs less than forming an entity.

DON'T GO OVERBOARD WITH EXPENSES

Most traders have reasonable business expenses (under $15,000). If they don't also report a significant Section 475 ordinary trading loss, it may not be enough to draw the attention of the IRS.

In their landmark court cases, Assaderaghi, Nelson, and Endicott triggered IRS exams with unrealistic business expenses on Schedule C and massive ordinary losses from trading on Form 4797 (Section 475 MTM) — all dependent on TTS qualification. The IRS denied TTS, and the deductions were not allowed on their respective returns.

Business traders should consider using a Schedule C for 2023 and forming a trading entity for 2024. A single-member or spousal-member LLC electing S-Corp treatment unlocks additional tax breaks like deductions for retirement plan contributions and health insurance premiums paid during the entity period.

DON'T BE AFRAID TO CLAIM TTS

The IRS may not be inclined to challenge a reasonable level of business expense deductions if a trader has significant trading gains. Our income-transfer strategy zeros out Schedule C, so it doesn't show a net loss. If a trader has small trading losses and business-trading expenses, it's probably not worth it for the IRS to audit the tax return. On the other hand, if a trader has a significant trading business loss comprised of substantial Schedule C expenses and Section 475 MTM ordinary trading losses, the IRS or the state may ask questions. Be prepared to defend TTS, as it's a requirement for Section 475 MTM ordinary loss treatment and is needed to deduct business-trading expenses.

Traders may consider soaking up ordinary trading losses under the excess business loss (EBL) limitation with a Roth IRA conversion executed before year-end. Consider it a way to convert an IRA inexpensively. (Chapter 8 contains more on Roth IRA conversions, and Chapter 9 shows examples of this tax planning strategy.)

After filing thousands of tax returns for business traders since the online revolution in 1997, the IRS has audited very few of our clients, and we received excellent results on those cases. Our audit percentages are considerably less than the national averages. We attribute this successful record to proper analysis of TTS, correct tax reporting techniques, accuracy and attention to detail, and detailed footnotes. (Read about footnotes in Chapter 6 and dealing with the IRS and states in Chapter 10.)

QUALIFYING CAN BE TRICKY

The IRS and states focus on verifiable factors such as volume of trades, frequency, and average holding period. Proving daily hours worked and business intention is hard, although traders should do their best to document those factors. Some brokers save login sessions, and traders should keep contemporaneous diaries. The biggest challenge is explaining how TTS fits in with a taxpayer's other jobs, businesses, and daily lifestyle. It's better if a trader's trading hours don't conflict with their other business activity or job hours.

CLOSE CALLS

The following are examples of business traders whose trader tax determination would be considered a close call. If a taxpayer is in a similar situation, they should proceed with caution when claiming TTS.

West Coast trader. Many West Coast traders operate a trading business early in the morning before commuting to their day jobs. Securities markets open at 6:30 a.m. PT, providing them with several hours of trading during peak market activity in the morning session. Many traders have browser-based trading platforms that they can easily access at their jobs, with or without employer approval. Many traders use mobile devices and apps to execute trades when outside their home office. These traders often spend considerable time on their trading business at lunch, on breaks, in the evenings, and on weekends. Again, the IRS can challenge claims about time, effort spent, and business intention, so ensure the number of trades, frequency, and holding periods are solid and verifiable. Traders should document trading purposes with a well-crafted business plan, document all time spent, and establish an excellent daily trend line in their calendars.

Trading futures, options, forex, cryptocurrencies, or other global markets. Many markets operate around different time zones; U.S.-based traders can trade for significant periods outside their weekday job hours. The IRS can question the number and purpose of late-night hours, so traders should keep their numbers strong.

Flextime employees and individuals transitioning into a full-time trading business. Many professionals work flexible hours and structure day jobs around trading and market hours. Many intend to leave their current jobs to become full-time traders. Many business owners have reliable employees running their businesses and focus most of their time on trading.

During the COVID-19 pandemic, many employees worked from their homes, allowing for easier coordination of trading and job duties.

An employee is operating a trading business on the side. Many traders want to retain employment and actively trade to increase income and financial independence. They intend to run a business and make a supplemental living trading. They don't plan to quit their job to pursue full-time trading, and that's okay.

Stay-at-home parent. Many stay-at-home parents trade to pursue their entrepreneurial dreams or help pay the bills while caring for their children (or elderly parents). The IRS can doubt a trader's sincerity here, so traders should avoid sporadic lapses in executing trades and keep the trading business open for several years. Profitability helps, too. Traders should be professional in their approach and discipline.

Early retiree. While many people may decide to retire from their full-time careers around age 62, they want to stay busy and enhance their income. Retirees seek new income opportunities, and a trading business can be ideal. Many retirees self-direct their retirement funds and investment accounts, so they already have one foot in the trading business door. Others are offered early retirement or are laid off in their 50s and may decide to pursue a trading business. Many believe they have insufficient retirement assets and seek to enhance their returns by trading.

The IRS tends to be skeptical of retirees, thinking they are retired from the business entirely. Since that's untrue, taxpayers must impress the IRS with their professionalism and business acumen.

An unemployed individual. While considering new employment opportunities, many out-of-work individuals are attracted to the ease and possibility of a trading business. Most people already have the necessities — a computer, mobile devices, and wireless access— in place. There's no need to obtain an office lease, hire employees, get a professional license, and attract customers.

Even so, traders can also lose money very fast. It's best to attain a trading education first; plenty of free and premium educational resources are available. In most states, a trader can continue to collect unemployment benefits while trading because trading is considered an investment activity rather than a job by most unemployment agencies. (Perhaps some states don't allow this, but we don't know of any at the time of this writing.) In most states, traders can also form a trading entity without jeopardizing those benefits. However, we advise against taking compensation from the trading entity, as that is a conflict. It's wise for taxpayers to check with their federal, state, or other unemployment benefits/disability benefits provider.

Some traders find new jobs and give up trading after experiencing losses or low profitability. A short period in a trading business can negate TTS in the eyes of the IRS. In Chen vs. Commissioner — another landmark tax court case denying TTS — Chen only traded for three months before losing his trading money, thereby exiting his trading activity. Chen kept his job during his three months of trading, so his case differs from that of an unemployed trader. However, this case

indefinitely (20 years before the TCJA changes). The NOL deduction is limited to 80% of the subsequent year's taxable income. TCJA's 2018 excess business loss (EBL) limitation was $500,000 (married) /$250,000 (other taxpayers). Add the excess over the EBL threshold to an NOL carryforward. (See Chapters 7 and 9.)

The inflation-adjusted 2023 EBL threshold is $578,000 (married)/$289,000 (other taxpayers), and the 2024 EBL threshold is $610,000 (married)/$305,000 (other taxpayers).

The 2020 CARES Act for COVID-19 relief suspended TCJA's EBL rules for 2018, 2019, and 2020 and allowed five-year NOL carrybacks during these years only. For example, CARES allowed taxpayers to carry back a 2020 NOL to 2015. The NOL and EBL rules apply again from 2021 through 2025. Other recent tax laws extended EBL further to 2028.

TCJA introduced a significant tax benefit — the 20% qualified business income (QBI) deduction. QBI includes TTS Section 475 ordinary income and losses, net of TTS trading expenses, but excludes capital gains and losses, forex income, swap income, dividends, and interest income. Trading is a "specified service trade or business" (SSTB), so a taxable income cap and phase-out range apply. (See Chapter 17.) If your taxable income exceeds the QBI threshold, you won't get a QBI deduction.

There are many nuances and misconceptions about Section 475 MTM, and learning the rules is essential. For example, taxpayers can segregate investment positions on a contemporaneous basis that aren't subject to Section 475 MTM treatment. At year-end, they can defer unrealized gains on properly segregated investments. Taxpayers can have the best of both worlds — ordinary gains and losses on trading and deferral with lower long-term capital gains tax rates on segregated investment positions. (I address concerns about segregation later in the chapter.)

A TTS trader can only elect Section 475 on securities to retain lower 60/40 capital gains rates on Section 1256 contracts (commodities). Many accountants and traders confuse TTS and Section 475. They are two different but connected things. TTS is like an undergraduate university, and Section 475 is like graduate school.

SECTION 475 IS TAX-LOSS INSURANCE

Because Section 475 MTM allows ordinary losses, it generates significant tax breaks immediately rather than being stuck with large capital-loss carryovers to subsequent tax years.

There are other losses to worry about, including wash-sale loss adjustments. Day and swing traders inevitably trigger many wash-sale (WS) loss adjustments amounting to tens or hundreds of thousands of dollars. Create a WS loss when you take a loss on a security and repurchase it within 30 days (after or before).

A Section 475 election exempts the TTS trader from wash-sale loss adjustments on securities. WS defers tax losses to replacement positions. If that happens around year-end, it might create a phantom taxable income because it defers tax losses to the subsequent year. See more information on wash-sale loss adjustments in Chapter 4. WS is the number one worry of securities traders.

Section 475 MTM also reports year-end unrealized gains and losses as marked-to-market, which means one must impute sales for all open trading positions at year-end using year-end prices. Many traders have no open trading positions at year-end, anyway. They report realized and unrealized gains and losses, like Section 1256, which has MTM built in by default — but don't confuse Section 1256 with Section 475.

We coined the term "tax-loss insurance" for Section 475 because if a taxpayer's trading house burns down, he can deduct Section 475 trading losses immediately and get a huge tax break (refund or lower tax bill). It's a free insurance premium on securities because short-term capital gains use ordinary tax rates like Section 475 MTM. But, Section 475 ordinary losses can be deducted in the current year, up to the EBL limitation, offsetting any other taxable ordinary income, which could generate immediate tax benefits and refunds. Capital losses do not offer the same help due to the $3,000 net capital loss deduction limitation.

It's entirely different with Section 1256 contracts, where the tax-loss insurance premium is expensive. Electing Section 475 on Section 1256 contracts means taxpayers must give up the lower Section 1256 60/40 capital gains tax rates in exchange for ordinary income rates. Plus, there is a Section 1256 loss carryback election (discussed later). QBI requires Section 475, but the trader might exceed the QBI income threshold.

There are more nuances to consider as well.

CAPITAL-LOSS CARRYOVER MISCONCEPTIONS

Many traders mistakenly think they can only utilize $3,000 of capital-loss carryovers annually. They worry it can take a lifetime to use up their capital losses. They don't realize subsequent-year net capital gains offset the capital-loss carryover without limitation. When considering the MTM election, it is important to plan how they will be able to use the capital-loss carryover. If they remain in capital gains treatment, rather than electing Section 475 MTM ordinary income, taxable capital gains in subsequent years can be reduced by the capital-loss carryover. The net $3,000 capital loss deduction is against non-capital gains income, or essentially any income that makes it to the first page of Form 1040.

If a taxpayer's capital-loss carryover to 2024 is $50,000 and their 2024 capital gains are $60,000, they can apply the $50,000 capital-loss carryover in full on Schedule D; their net capital gain would be $10,000. Conversely, if the 2024 capital gain is $35,000, the net capital loss before limitation would be $15,000 ($35,000 minus the $50,000 carryover from 2023 to 2024). A $3,000 capital loss deduction is allowed against other income for 2024, so the remaining capital loss carried over to 2025 would be $12,000.

Capital-loss carryovers incurred before trading in a new pass-through entity will not be lost. The new entity can forgo a Section 475 election and pass through capital gains on a Schedule K-1 to individual tax returns (Schedule D), where individual capital-loss carryovers offset them. This strategy is the best way to climb out of a capital-loss carryover hole.

On the other hand, if the entity has losses during its first 75 days of inception, the taxpayer should move forward with the Section 475 election. The entity can then revoke Section 475 in the subsequent year to return to capital gains treatment to soak up the individual-level capital-loss carryovers, which never expire.

Using up capital-loss carryovers is critical. Proper Section 475 MTM election planning and entities are the answer. It pays to think out the nuances carefully and not make a blanket decision to skip Section 475, as that can cost a taxpayer big time!

SECTION 475 IS IDEAL FOR SECURITIES TRADERS

Securities traders should usually elect Section 475 MTM unless they already have significant capital-loss carryovers. Traders can't offset MTM ordinary trading gains with capital-loss carryovers. However, suppose a trader generates significant new trading losses before April 15, 2024. In that case, they might prefer to elect Section 475 MTM for 2024 by that sole proprietor election due date to have ordinary-loss treatment retroactive to Jan. 1, 2024. The trader can form a new entity afterward for a "do-over" to use the default capital gains treatment and get back on track by using up capital loss carryovers. Alternatively, the trader can revoke the entity's Section 475 election in the subsequent tax year.

SECTION 475 IS NOT ALWAYS WELL-SUITED FOR HEDGE FUNDS

Many hedge-fund managers find it restrictive to deal with the segregation of investment rules within Section 475 and skip the election. These managers have trouble determining trading positions vs. segregated investment positions, which they must do on the day they purchase a security. Many seek to defer capital gains at year-end to save their investors a tax bill, avoid investor redemption requests to pay related taxes, and seek lower long-term capital gains tax rates. Running afoul of the segregation rules can drag long-term positions into Section 475 MTM at year-end, meaning there will be no deferral and lower long-term capital gains tax rates. Hedge funds often generate trading gains and don't need the tax-loss insurance of Section 475 MTM. Many hedge fund investors want capital gains treatment to use up their capital loss carryovers; they don't like or expect Section 475 ordinary income.

However, hedge funds conducting short-term trading qualifying for TTS without investment positions should consider a Section 475 election.

SECTION 1256 BENEFITS

Section 1256 traders should generally not elect Section 475 because it overrides Section 1256; therefore, all trading gains would be subject to the short-term ordinary tax rate. In Section 1256, 60% of trading gains are considered long-term capital gains — even on day trades — taxed at lower tax rates (0%, 15%, and 20% in 2023 and 2024), and 40% are short-term capital gains taxed at ordinary tax rates (up to 37% in 2023 and 2024). The maximum 2023 and 2024 blended tax rate on Section 1256 contracts is 26.8% vs. 37% for securities at the ordinary rate, a meaningful 10.2% difference. The zero long-term rates correspond with the 10% and 12% ordinary brackets, with significant savings throughout the tax brackets. (See the Section 1256 tax table in the Green Trader Tax Center at https://greentradertax.com.)

Investors and TTS traders may elect to carry back Section 1256 contract losses for three tax years, applied against net Section 1256 contract gains on Form 6781. Check box D on top of Form 6781 before filing by the due date of the return, including extensions. Section 1256 contracts are also marked-to-market daily, but it's a different type of MTM than Section 475.

Suppose a trader of Section 1256 contracts incurs significant net trading losses before April 15, 2024. In that case, they may want to make the Section 475 election for commodities to lock in an ordinary loss. They might not have Section 1256 gains in the prior three tax years for a 1256 loss carryback election. Why not take the opportunity to lock in a sizable ordinary loss? A taxpayer can revoke Section 475 on commodities (including Section 1256 contracts) by the tax return due date in the following year to get back into lower 60/40 tax treatment on Section 1256 contracts. (See revocation below.)

DIGGING OUT OF A CAPITAL-LOSS HOLE

We design our trader tax strategies to prevent traders from falling into a hole of having unused capital losses. But many traders inevitably fall into that hole. This section focuses on how best to climb out using capital gains to soak up capital-loss carryovers and how not to dig a bigger hole by making a Section 475 MTM election. Traders must choose one tax treatment or the other, but at least they have some hindsight in this decision. Traders may choose the best tax treatment for the hindsight period — i.e., Jan. 1 to April 15, 2024.

Here are some examples. Suppose an individual taxpayer has a $50,000 capital-loss carryover going into 2024, and their Q1 2024 trading gains are $50,000. They should consider skipping the 2024 individual Section 475 MTM election since they want to offset their capital-loss carryover against current-year capital gains. The taxpayer is at breakeven, so it might be wise to form a new entity to elect Section 475 MTM for the remainder of 2024. It's best to select Section 475 when taxpayers have a clean slate — no material remaining capital loss carryovers and year-to-date realized losses and possibly unrealized capital losses on open positions. Trading in the entity during Q2, Q3, and Q4 will be ordinary gains and losses. Don't forget MTM's unrealized gains and losses on open positions at year-end.

Conversely, suppose a trader has an individual $50,000 capital-loss carryover going into 2024 and losses of $40,000 in Q1 2024. This trader should consider electing Section 475 MTM for ordinary loss treatment rather than digging a giant hole of unutilized capital losses. They can form a new entity for a "do-over" to return to capital gains treatment to use up the capital-loss carryovers. The entity has 75 days of additional hindsight once it commences trading. Ideally, the entity will generate capital gains to use up remaining capital-loss carryovers and put off the Section 475 MTM election until the following year.

There are many variations in these examples. No matter how much thought you put into it, there is still some risk in how it works out, and it won't always be a perfect result.

ELECTION PROCEDURES

Section 475 MTM is optional for individual TTS traders. In order to make the election, a trader must file a 2024 Section 475 election statement with their 2023 tax return or extension by April 15, 2024. Existing partnerships and S-Corps who must file a 2023 tax return should file a 2024 Section 475 election by March 15, 2024.

Election statement. The MTM election statement is a version of the following brief paragraph: "According to Section 475(f), the taxpayer at this moment elects to adopt the mark-to-market method of accounting for the tax year ending Dec. 31, 2024, and subsequent tax years. The election applies to the following trade or business: Trader in Securities as a sole proprietor (for securities only and not commodities/Section 1256 contracts)."

If traders expect a loss in trading Section 1256 contracts, they can modify the parenthetical reference to say, "for securities and commodities/Section 1256 contracts." But remember, the lower 60/40 tax rates on Section 1256 contracts will no longer apply to futures trades. If the taxpayer trades in an entity, they should delete "as a sole proprietor" in the statement.

Form 3115 filing. Don't forget an essential second step: Existing taxpayers complete the election process by filing Form 3115 (change of accounting method) with the election-year tax return. A 2023 MTM election filed by April 18, 2023, is perfected on Form 3115 filed with 2023 tax returns — by the due date of the return, including extensions.

You must submit Form 3115 in duplicate — one goes with Form 1040 or the entity tax return filing, and the second goes to the IRS national office. There's no fee for filing Form 3115, and the election is automatic. That means the IRS will not confirm this election statement or the Form 3115 filing.

We suggest you include an additional document with the filing of Form 3115. A perjury statement affirming you filed the Section 475 MTM election on time. The IRS system for recording Section 475 elections needs improvement, which is why the perjury statement is a good idea.

Some traders change their minds after filing their Section 475 election statement and want to skip the Form 3115 filing. That's wrong and incumbent on them to perfect the election. One proper way to cut the perfection of a Section 475 MTM election is to assume the non-qualification of TTS. But the facts must bear that out. It's essential to be consistent and credible with the IRS in everything involving TTS and Section 475. (See "Null and Void and Suspended Elections" later in this chapter.)

INTERNAL ELECTIONS FOR NEW TAXPAYERS

The Section 475 election procedure is different for "new taxpayers" like a new entity. Within 75 days of inception, a new taxpayer may file the Section 475 election statement internally in its records. The date of the state's certificate of LLC organization is the inception date.

The new entity does not have to submit Form 3115 because it's adopting Section 475 from inception rather than changing its accounting method. One way to file an internal resolution is for the taxpayer to send themself an email resolution (election), which has a timestamp for proof of a timely election.

Individuals are "new taxpayers" only if they have never filed an income tax return before (i.e., a trader aged 18). A new trader is not necessarily a new taxpayer for purposes of a 475 election.

SECTION 481(A) ADJUSTMENT

Form 3115 includes a section for reporting a Section 481(a) adjustment required when making an accounting change. The remainder of the multi-page Form 3115 relates to tax law, code sections, etc.

When changing to Section 475 MTM for 2024, a trader's section 481(a) adjustment is the unrealized capital gain or loss on TTS positions as of Dec. 31, 2023, the prior tax year. If a taxpayer didn't have TTS as of December 31, 2023, there is no Section 481(a) adjustment to report on the 2024 return. In other words, the only positions included in Section 481(a) adjustment are trading positions; they do not include segregated investment positions. If the first year of TTS qualification is 2024, then 2023 year-end positions are investments.

A total section 481(a) loss is deductible, whereas a taxpayer must prorate a section 481(a) gain of more than $50,000 over four years. If the 481(a) income is $50,000 or less, the IRS permits the taxpayer to elect to report the entire gain in the first year. For different reasons, income proration can be favorable to taxpayers — but don't forget to report these deferred items in later tax years. The taxpayer must accelerate the proration and report all remaining deferred gains as taxable if they exit TTS trading before the deferred portion has all been taxed.

Section 1256 contract traders don't have to worry about a 481(a) adjustment since MTM is the default gain loss calculation for those trades.

For a 2023 Section 475 MTM election for securities, the 481(a) adjustment is reportable as a Jan. 1, 2023, on the 2023 Form 4797 Part II, along with MTM trading gains and losses for 2023 (which starts the year at market values for cost basis). Some trade accounting software makes a 481(a) adjustment calculation easier.

ELECTION TO REVOKE SECTION 475

The IRS makes revocation a free and easy process, mirroring the Section 475 election and an automatic change of accounting procedure for existing taxpayers. One drawback is that taxpayers cannot re-elect Section 475 for five years after revocation.

Before this rule change, the Section 475 revocation procedure cost several thousand dollars in filing fees (close to $7,000 for hedge funds), and the outcome was uncertain since it required advanced consent from the IRS. Few traders opted for revocation; most used other options like suspension or exit.

The new revocation procedure is like the election procedure. An existing individual must file a 2024 notification statement of revocation with the IRS by April 15, 2024 (March 15, 2024, for partnerships and S-Corps). The second step is to file 2024 Form 3115 to revoke Section 475 with the 2024 tax return. There is no IRS fee.

Many traders "suspend" TTS and the related Section 475 election. By disqualifying themselves for TTS, they revert to being investors who may not use Section 475 as of the TTS disqualification date. TTS business expense treatment and use of Section 475 MTM is put on hold until the trader re-qualifies again (if ever) for TTS.

Taxpayers appreciate having this choice to revoke Section 475 instead of leaving it suspended on their returns if they elected it as a sole proprietor trader. See New IRS Rules Allow Free & Easy Section 475 Revocation, https://tinyurl.com/475-revocation.

NULL, VOID, AND SUSPENDED 475 ELECTIONS

We had discussions with the IRS regarding Section 475 MTM elections for traders who never qualified for TTS or those who exited with a valid Section 475 MTM election. Here's one example: A new trader was unsure if they would qualify for TTS in 2023, but they filed the 2023 Section 475 MTM election by April 18, 2023. But they didn't end up qualifying for TTS in 2023. Therefore, the election was "null and void," and they skipped filing a 2023 Form 3115. If they want Section 475 for 2024, they need to start fresh and file a 2024 Section 475 MTM election statement by April 15, 2024.

Suppose an existing sole proprietor business trader elected and used Section 475 MTM in 2023 and stopped trading on Dec. 31, 2023. They should consider filing an election to revoke Section 475 by April 15, 2024, effective Jan. 1, 2024.

Conversely, suppose they stop trading on June 30, 2024 — after the date to submit a 2024 revocation. This person can discontinue using TTS and 475, which is suspended as of June 30, 2024. They can make a revocation election by April 15, 2025. They will use Section 475 until June 30, 2024, and the realization (cash) method for the remainder of 2024.

AN EXTENSION FOR SECTION 475 IS UNLIKELY

If you miss April 15, 2024, the 2024 Section 475 election deadline, you can consider a private letter ruling (PLR) for a six-month extension under Section 9100 relief. However, it's doubtful it will win IRS approval. The IRS denied PLRs for Section 475 MTM extension requests in the past except for one. The Vines vs. Commissioner case is the only one where the taxpayer prevailed. Vines, an attorney and trader, had several million dollars of trading losses before the Section 475 MTM election deadline of April 15. He did not know about Section 475 MTM, did not trade after the MTM election deadline, and did not use hindsight to prejudice the IRS. Vines had a perfect set of factors that other taxpayers would unlikely duplicate.

A PLR is an expensive process. To win a PLR on a Section 475 MTM extension procedure, a trader must prove they did not use "hindsight." Examples of hindsight are having a capital-loss carryover to start the year, having unrealized capital losses, having commingling investment positions, trading Section 1256 contracts with lower 60/40 capital gains rates, or having capital gains at the beginning of the year turn into trading losses after the 475 MTM election date. A taxpayer must also show "unusual and compelling" facts and circumstances, which is challenging.

A better solution is to form a new entity and file the 475 MTM election statement internally within 75 days of inception. But this won't help with pre-entity losses if a taxpayer misses the MTM election on April 15. Many new traders don't begin trading until after April 15; an entity is wise if they want Section 475 MTM.

IRS CAN DENY ORDINARY-LOSS TREATMENT

Suppose traders don't follow Section 475 MTM election steps by the respective deadlines. In that case, the IRS may seek to deny ordinary-loss treatment, thereby taking away Section 475 MTM tax-loss insurance and a QBI deduction on gains.

Traders must carefully apply Section 475 MTM on their tax returns using Form 4797. In several tax court cases, the IRS has debated TTS. Still, it will forcefully deny ordinary trading loss treatment if the taxpayer elected Section 475 MTM too late or botched and couldn't prove the election. This result was evident in the October 2015 Poppe tax court ruling covered in Chapter 11. Follow the two-step election process to the letter of the law.

SEGREGATION OF INVESTMENTS

Suppose a trader holds investment positions in equities and trades substantially identical securities in equities or equity options using TTS and Section 475. The IRS could recharacterize trades as investments or vice versa, whichever suits them best. For example, the IRS could reclassify an investment position in Apple equity currently deferred for long-term capital gains into Section 475 MTM ordinary income at year-end. Alternatively, the IRS could recharacterize Section 475 MTM ordinary losses on Apple options as capital losses, triggering a $3,000 capital loss limitation.

Traders with an overlap between investing and trading activity should consider ring-fencing TTS/475 trading into an entity and conducting their investment activity individually. That solution would fix the potential IRS problem.

Here's an example: A taxpayer owns an investment portfolio of equities. They leverage their investments using portfolio margining to trade equity options around those investment positions to manage risk on the portfolio and collect option premiums. They are not selling naked options because they hold equity investments and trades in the same brokerage account. They must choose between using Section 475 versus portfolio margining, or ring-fence trading into an LLC/partnership or S-Corp.

475 FIXES WASH SALES WITH IRAS FOR TTS TRADES

If there is an overlap of positions traded in taxable accounts vs. IRA investments, the trader must avoid triggering permanent wash-sale losses throughout the year. Suppose a trader takes a loss in a taxable account and buys back a substantially identical securities position 30 days before or after in an IRA account. In that case, the wash-sale loss disenfranchisement becomes permanent.

To avoid such overlap, traders can fix this problem with a "do not invest" list. One strategy is to trade equities and equity options in taxable accounts and invest in ETFs and mutual funds in IRAs.

TTS traders can make a Section 475 election to do away with wash sales between trades and the IRAs, so overlap is not a problem.

Consider all IRA accounts for married filing joint, including traditional IRAs, Roth IRAs, rollover IRAs, and SEP IRAs. Do not include 401(k) or solo 401(k) plans.

Most traders are unaware of the nuances of triggering permanent wash sales between taxable and IRA accounts. IRS rules for broker-issued 1099-Bs have a narrow view of wash sales; they call for wash-sale loss adjustments on "identical symbols" for one account. Conversely, IRS wash sale rules for taxpayers have a broader view: Calculate wash sales on "substantially identical positions" (between equities and equity options) on all individual brokerage accounts, including IRAs. Consider using trade accounting software compliant with IRS wash-sale rules for taxpayers.

Section 475 is a consequential election for TTS traders with many advantages, but consider the nuances and your circumstances first.

Chapter 3

Tax Treatment of Financial Products

Tax treatment of financial products affects investors, traders, and hedge funds. But sadly, many taxpayers overlook essential differences in tax treatment for these groups, resulting in tax overpayments. Education is key. This chapter contains valuable information about how to treat the various instruments come tax time. We cover U.S. and international equities, U.S. futures, and other Section 1256 contracts, options, ETFs, ETNs, forex, precious metals, foreign futures, cryptocurrencies, and swap contracts.

It's important to distinguish between securities vs. Section 1256 contracts with lower 60/40 capital gains rates vs. other financial products such as forex or swaps with ordinary income or loss treatment. Various elections are available to change tax treatment.

DON'T RELY SOLELY ON 1099-Bs

One might expect that broker-issued 1099-Bs would handle all these issues, but for some tax treatments, they do not. For example, some brokers categorize CBOE-listed options on volatility ETNs (i.e., VXX) as securities. Still, there is substantial authority to treat these CBOE-listed options like VXX as "non-equity options" included in Section 1256, which might be more tax advantageous.

Broker compliance rules differ from those taxpayers should follow on wash-sale loss adjustments on securities. How you report the activity on your tax return depends on your facts, circumstances, and elections. There is no way for every broker to police all their clients' elections, qualification for trader tax status (TTS), and whether they have filed an election for Section 475 MTM on time. Brokers should issue 1099-Bs for the "everyman," not based on each taxpayer's facts, circumstances, and elections filed. Therefore, it is imperative that taxpayers review the 1099-Bs entirely and only use the information if it agrees with their situation.

Some financial products like spot forex are not "covered securities" for 1099-B issuance. Some U.S. cryptocurrency exchanges issue a Form 1099-K (Payment Card and Third-Party Network Transactions) to investors who reach a certain threshold of transactions. For 2023, some U.S. cryptocurrency exchanges are issuing a 1099-MISC or 1099-B.

Brokers issue Form 1099-Bs for securities and Section 1256 contracts to investors and traders. Recent tax legislation beefs up tax compliance and reporting for cryptocurrencies.

CAPITAL GAINS VS. ORDINARY INCOME

Most financial instruments — including equities, futures, options, ETFs, ETNs, precious metals, and cryptocurrencies held as capital assets — are subject to capital gains treatment. However, some financial products, such as U.S. futures, qualify as Section 1256 contracts with lower 60/40 capital gains rates. The distinction between typical capital gains and 60/40 capital gains treatment makes a big difference. The capital-loss limitation is a problem for traders and investors who may have trouble using large capital-loss carryovers in subsequent tax years. Forex contracts and swap contracts are subject to ordinary gain or loss treatment by default. Traders with TTS and a Section 475 MTM election have ordinary-loss treatment, which is more likely to generate tax savings or refunds sooner. Some financial products don't qualify for a Section 475 election, including forex, cryptocurrencies, and ETNs structured as prepaid forward contracts. ETNs structured as debt instruments are securities eligible for Section 475 treatment.

SECURITIES

Securities traders have ordinary tax rates on short-term capital gains, wash-sale loss adjustments, capital-loss limitations, and accounting challenges.

Securities include

- U.S. and international equities (stocks)
- U.S. and foreign equity (stock) options
- narrow-based indexes (an index made up of nine or fewer securities)
- options on narrow-based indexes
- securities ETFs structured as registered investment companies (RIC)
- options on securities ETF RICs
- commodities ETFs structured as publicly traded partnerships (PTP)
- volatility ETNs structured as debt instruments
- bonds
- mutual funds
- single-stock futures

The IRS taxes securities transactions when a taxpayer closes an open trade — hence the term "realization method." Taxpayers can defer capital gains by holding open securities positions at year-end. With "tax-loss harvesting," investors sell to realize losses before year-end 2023. Do not re-enter those positions within 31 days; otherwise, the planned loss might defer to 2024 as a wash-sale loss adjustment. Wash sales during the year can be okay, providing you close them out before year-end.

Short-term capital gains (STCG) use ordinary tax rates, with progressive tax brackets currently up to 37% for 2023 and 2024. Long-term capital gains (LTCG) rates are significantly lower and apply to sales of securities held for 12 months or more. The LTCG rates are 0% for the 10% and 12% ordinary brackets, 15% in the middle brackets, and 20% in the top 37% bracket.

The 1099-B displays each opening and closing securities trade and wash-sale loss adjustment with the tax realization method. Report those details on Form 8949, which feeds into Schedule D, where short- and long-term capital gains rates apply. (See accounting and tax reporting for securities in Chapter 4.)

The mark-to-market (MTM) accounting method is different from the realization method. MTM also reports unrealized capital gains and losses at year-end by imputing sales of open positions using year-end prices. Traders eligible for TTS can elect Section 475 MTM ordinary gain or loss on securities and commodities. Section 475 securities trades are exempt from wash-sale loss adjustments and the $3,000 capital loss limitation. Qualified business income (QBI) includes net Section 475 gains, so TTS traders can get a 20% QBI deduction if they are under the income cap. (A timely 475 MTM election is critical, see Chapter 2.)

SECTION 1256 CONTRACTS

Section 1256 contracts enjoy lower 60/40 capital gains tax rates, summary tax reporting, easier mark-to-market (MTM) accounting, and a Section 1256 loss carryback election.

Section 1256 contracts include:

- U.S. regulated futures contracts (RFCs) and options on U.S. RFCs
- U.S. broad-based indexes made up of 10 or more underlying securities – also known as stock index futures
- options on U.S. broad-based indexes
- foreign futures if granted Section 1256 treatment in an IRS revenue ruling (lists are online at https://greentradertax.com/tax-treatment-for-foreign-futures/)
- non-equity options (a catchall)
- CBOE-listed options on commodity ETF widely-held publicly traded partnerships (PTP)
- CBOE-listed options on precious metals ETF publicly traded trusts (PTT)
- CBOE-listed options on volatility ETN prepaid forward contracts
- forward forex contracts with the opt-out election into Section 1256(g) on the major pairs for which futures trade (we make a case for spot forex, too)
- forex OTC options (Wright court)

Section 1256 contracts have lower 60/40 capital gains tax rates: 60% (including day trades) subject to lower long-term capital gains rates and 40% taxed as short-term capital gains using the ordinary rate. At the maximum tax bracket for 2023 and 2024, the blended 60/40 rate is 26.8% — 10.2%, lower than the highest regular bracket of 37%.

There are significant tax savings throughout the income brackets. The LTCG rate in the lowest two ordinary brackets is 0%. (See our table at https://tinyurl.com/section-1256.) Regular state tax rates apply because they do not include a long-term rate.

Section 1256 contracts are marked-to-market (MTM) daily. For tax purposes, MTM reports both realized activity throughout the year and unrealized gains and losses on open trading positions at year-end.

With MTM and summary reporting, brokers issue simple one-page 1099-Bs reporting "aggregate profit or loss on contracts" by reporting both realized and unrealized gains and losses. Report that amount on Form 6781 Part I, which breaks the net 1256 gain loss down by the 60/40 split and then moves the amounts to Schedule D capital gains/losses.

There is a Section 1256 loss carryback election. Rather than use the 1256 loss in the current year, taxpayers may deduct 1256 losses on amended tax return filings, applied against Section 1256 gains only. (Using Form 1045 is better than 1040X; the IRS issues the refund faster, and the process is less complicated.) It's a three-year carryback; unused amounts carry forward, and it's the only remaining carryback opportunity for traders. (For details on executing this 1256 loss carryback election, see Chapter 6.)

Section 1256 traders should also learn about the mixed straddle election and hedging rules in Section 1256(d) and (e), as discussed in Form 6781. Offsetting positions between Section 1256 contracts and securities can generate tax complications under certain circumstances involving the hedging rule. The IRS is concerned about traders reporting Section 1256 MTM unrealized losses and deferring unrealized gains on related securities positions.

EXCHANGE-TRADED FUNDS

Securities, commodities, and precious metals ETFs use different structures, and tax treatment varies.

Securities ETFs usually are regulated investment companies (RICs). Like mutual fund RICs, securities ETFs pass through their underlying ordinary and qualifying dividends to investors. Selling a securities ETF is a sale of a security, calling for short- and long-term capital gains tax treatment using the realization method. A securities ETF is a security, so wash-sale loss adjustments or Section 475 apply if elected.

Commodities/futures ETFs. Regulators do not permit commodities/futures ETFs to use the RIC structure, so publicly traded partnerships (PTPs) are how they are usually structured. Commodities/futures ETFs issue annual Schedule K-1s passing through their underlying Section 1256 tax treatment to investors and other taxable items. Selling a commodities ETF is a sale of a security and calls for short- and long-term capital gains tax treatment using the realization method. Wash-sale loss adjustments, or Section 475 apply if elected, because a commodities ETF PTP is widely held.

Taxpayers invested in commodities/futures ETFs may need to make cost-basis adjustments on Form 8949 to capital gains and losses, ensuring they don't double-count the Schedule K-1 pass-through items. For example, if the K-1 passes through Section 1256 income to Form 6781, the taxpayer should also add that income to the cost basis on Form 8949. Otherwise, they will double count the income, causing an overstatement of tax liability. Form 1099-Bs and trade accounting programs do not make these cost-basis adjustments from K-1 income/loss, so adjust Form 8949 accordingly.

Master limited partnerships (MLPs) are PTPs issuing Schedule K-1s to investors with pass-through income. Purchasing a PTP with business dealings, such as oil and gas operations, in a retirement account will probably cause unrelated business taxable income and tax (UBIT) and a Form 990 filing requirement since the K-1 passes through business income. See our blog post, Retirement Plan Investments in Publicly Traded Partnerships Generate Tax Bills, https://tinyurl.com/retirement-ptp.

Physically backed precious metals ETFs. These ETFs may not use the RIC structure either. Although they could use the PTP structure, they usually choose the publicly traded trust (PTT) structure (also known as a grantor trust). A PTT issues an annual Schedule K-1, passing through tax treatment to the investor, which, in this case, is the "collectibles" capital gains rate on sales of physically backed precious metals (such as gold bullion). Selling a precious metal ETF is selling precious metal, which is a collectible. If taxpayers hold collectibles over one year (long-term), sales are taxed at the "collectibles" capital gains tax rate — capped at 28%. (If the ordinary rate is lower, use it.) That 28% rate is higher than the top long-term capital gains rate of 20% (2023 and 2024). Short-term capital gains use the ordinary tax rates. Physically backed precious metals ETFs are not securities, so they are not subject to wash-sale loss adjustments or Section 475 if elected. (For more information, see our blog Tax Treatment for Precious Metals at https://tinyurl.com/rrmbg87, which includes a discussion on all sorts of precious metal ETFs.)

OPTIONS

Options cover the gamut of tax treatment. They are a derivative of their underlying instrument and generally have the same tax treatment. For example, equity options are a derivative of the underlying equity, and both are securities. Tax treatment for options is diverse, including simple (outright) and complex trades with multiple legs.

Options taxed as securities:

- equity (stock) options
- options on narrow-based indexes
- options on securities ETFs RIC

Options taxed as 1256 contracts:

- non-equity options (a catchall)
- options on U.S. regulated futures contracts and broad-based indexes
- CBOE-listed options on commodity ETF publicly traded partnerships
- CBOE-listed options on precious metals ETF publicly traded trusts
- CBOE-listed options on volatility ETN prepaid forward contracts
- forex OTC options (Wright appeals court)

Generally, options listed on a commodities exchange, labeled a "qualified board or exchange" (QBE), are a 1256 contract unless the reference is a single stock or a narrow-based stock index.

For options taxed as securities, wash-sale loss rules apply between substantially identical positions in securities, which means between equity and equity options, such as Apple stock and Apple stock options, at different expiration dates. (These are IRS WS rules for taxpayers, which are broader than for brokers on 1099-Bs). Because wash-sale loss rules only apply to securities, they do not apply to options taxed as Section 1256 contracts.

Simple vs. complex options trades. Simple option trading strategies like buying and selling call-and-put options are known as outrights. Complex options trades known as option spreads include multi-legged offsetting positions like iron condors; butterfly spreads; vertical, horizontal, and diagonal spreads; and debit and credit spreads.

Tax treatment for outright option trades is relatively straightforward. However, complex options trades trigger a bevy of IRS rules geared toward preventing taxpayers from tax avoidance schemes: deducting losses and expenses from the losing side of the trade in the current tax year while deferring income on the offsetting winning position until a subsequent tax year.

Three things can happen with outright option trades:

1. Trade option (closing transaction): Trading call and put equity options held as a capital asset is taxed the same as trading underlying equities. Taxpayers should report proceeds, cost basis, wash-sale loss adjustments, and net capital gain or loss and holding period (short-term vs. long-term held more than 12 months) from realized transactions only on Form 8949. Section 1256 options are reported in summary form with MTM on Form 6781.

2. Option expires (lapses): The above scenario can have a minor twist. Rather than realizing a dollar amount on the closing out of the options trade, the closeout price is zero since the option expires worthless. Use zero for the realized proceeds or cost basis, depending on whether you're the "writer "or "holder" of the option and if it's a call or put. Use common sense — collecting premium on the option trade counts as proceeds; therefore, the corresponding worthless exercise represents zero cost basis in this realized transaction. For guidance on entering option transactions as expired on Form 8949, read IRS Pub. 550 – Capital Gains And Losses: Options.

3. Exercise the option: This is where tax treatment becomes more complicated. Exercising an option is not a realized gain or loss transaction; it's a stepping stone to a subsequent realized gain or loss transaction on the underlying financial instrument acquired. The original option transaction

amount is absorbed (adjusted) into the following financial instrument cost basis, or net proceeds amount. IRS Pub. 550 states:

"If you exercise a call, add its cost to the basis of the stock you bought. If you exercise a put, reduce your amount realized on the sale of the underlying stock by the price of the put when figuring your gain or loss. Any gain or loss on the sale of the underlying stock is long-term or short-term, depending on your holding period for the underlying stock.

"If a put you write is exercised and you buy the underlying stock, decrease your basis in the stock by the amount you received for the put …

"If a call you write is exercised and you sell the underlying stock, increase your amount realized on the sale of the stock by the amount you received for the call when figuring your gain or loss."

Some brokers interpret these IRS rules differently, which can lead to confusion when attempting to reconcile broker-issued Form 1099-Bs to trade accounting software. A few brokers may reduce proceeds when they should add the amount to the cost basis.

Exercising an option gets to the basics of what an option is all about: It's the right, but not the obligation, to purchase or sell a financial instrument at a fixed "strike price" by expiration date. Exercise may happen at any time until the option lapses. An investor can have an in-the-money option before the expiration date and choose not to execute it but hold or sell it before expiration.

The holding period for long-term capital gains: When a trader exercises an equity option, the option holding period becomes irrelevant, and the holding period for the equity begins anew. The holding period of the option doesn't help achieve a long-term capital gain 12-month holding period on the subsequent sale of the equity. When an option is closed or lapsed, the option holding period dictates short- or long-term capital gains treatment, with these exceptions recapped in IRS Pub. 550:

"Buying a put option is generally treated as a short sale, and the exercise, sale, or expiration of the put is a closing of the short sale. If you have held the underlying stock for one year or less when you buy the put, any gain on the put's exercise, sale, or expiration is a short-term capital gain. The same is true if you buy the underlying stock after you buy the put but before its exercise, sale, or expiration."

For more information about tax treatment for options, including complex trades, straddles, offsetting positions, and wash sales on options, see our blog post Tax Treatment for Trading Options, https://tinyurl.com/gtt-options. Trade accounting software generally does not automatically account for offsetting positions on complex trades, so be prepared to make manual adjustments. I recommend Section 475 for complex options traders to avoid complications with offsetting option positions.

FOREX

Forex refers to the foreign exchange market (also known as the "Interbank" market), where participants trade currencies, including spot, forwards, or over-the-counter (OTC) option contracts. Forex differs from trading currency-regulated futures contracts (RFCs). Currency RFCs are Section 1256 contracts reported on Form 6781 with lower 60/40 capital gains tax treatment.

Forex tax treatment. By default, forex transactions start off receiving ordinary gain or loss treatment as Section 988 (foreign currency transactions) dictates. The excellent news is that Section 988 ordinary losses offset ordinary income in full and are not subject to the $3,000 capital loss limitation — that's a welcome relief for many new forex traders who have initial losses and offset the losses against wage and other income.

Section 988 allows investors and business traders — but not manufacturers — to internally file a contemporaneous "capital gains election" to opt out of Section 988 into capital gain or loss treatment. Generate capital gains to use up capital loss carryovers, which otherwise may go wasted for years.

The capital gains election on forex forwards allows the trader to use Section 1256(g) treatment with lower 60/40 capital gains rates on major currency pairs if the trader doesn't take or make delivery of the underlying currency. A major currency pair is a forex pair that also trades as a regulated futures contract on U.S. futures exchanges. There are lists of currency pairs that trade on U.S. futures exchanges available online (search FX products on CME).

Spot vs. forwards. Most online trading platforms and brokers only offer forex spot contracts. Because guidance from the IRS isn't clear, most retail off-exchange forex traders are unsure how to handle spot forex. Our extensive work in this area has led us to believe that, in many cases, spot forex can be treated like forex forwards, qualifying for lower 60/40 tax rates in Section 1256(g) on major currency pairs only with the capital gains election. These tax rates may be desirable if you have significant trading gains on spot forex contracts. We lay out a case for Section 1256(g) treatment on spot forex transactions, with certain conditions and restrictions. It's essential to use proper tax return footnote disclosure. (See blog post referenced below.)

Forex tax reporting. Brokers provide details and summary reporting for forex trades; most offer helpful online tax reports. Spot forex brokers aren't supposed to issue Form 1099-Bs at tax time. Section 988 provides for realized gain or loss, whereas, with a capital gains election on major pairs into Section 1256(g), MTM gain loss calculation rules apply.

Investors report Section 988 transactions in summary form on line 8(z), "other income" of 2023 Schedule 1 (Form 1040). Watch out for negative taxable income caused by forex losses without TTS; you might waste some losses. (TTS forex traders use Form 4797 Part II instead, and the negative income may generate an NOL carryover depending on the taxpayer's income from other sources.) Section 1256(g) treatment uses Form 6781, just like other Section 1256 contracts.

Rollover trades. Spot contracts clear within two days, whereas forward contracts clear over two days. If a trader wants to stay in a spot trade longer than two days, the broker offers a "rollover trade," which technically is a realized sale and purchase of a new position (but not all brokers treat it that way). Forex spot traders don't take delivery of foreign exchange.

Forex brokers handle rollover interest and rollover trades differently. In most cases, it's not an interest expense but rather part of trading gain or loss.

The Section 988 opt-out election. Make the Section 988 opt-out election by filing it internally (meaning you don't have to file an election statement with the IRS) on a contemporaneous basis (meaning the IRS does not allow hindsight — the election is effective from the date made going forward). Section 988 talks about the election on every trade, but you can also make a "good to cancel" election, which is more practical. You can make the election and withdraw it throughout the year.

Forex OTC options: Few retail traders can trade forex OTC options. Per TaxNotes, "Representing a turnaround from what was understood to be prior law, the Sixth Circuit Court of Appeals held Jan. 7, 2016, in the Wright decision, that over-the-counter foreign currency options are subject to mark-to-market accounting under section 1256." In 2007, the IRS barred forex OTC options from Section 1256. (I cover the Wright decision in A Case For Retail Forex Traders Using Section 1256(g) Lower 60/40 Tax Rates, https://tinyurl.com/forex-1256g.)

A word of caution: Forex trading losses can become wasted for non-TTS traders who don't elect out of Section 988 and have negative taxable income. Forex losses become a part of NOL for those who qualify for TTS, but investors don't have NOL treatment. Investors with no other source of income may be better off electing out of Section 988, so their forex losses can be classified as capital-loss carryovers and not wasted forever. Remember, the effective date of the election is as of the date made and going forward.

Physically held currency: Tax treatment varies when holding physical foreign currency. Section 988 rules apply, but the IRS does not permit a capital gains opt-out election as it does on forex contracts. That means investing in physical currency is an ordinary gain or loss treatment in Section 988.

Losses are not deductible for the personal use of currency, such as on vacation, while gains are considered capital gains. Section 988 and the capital gains election don't apply to the private use of foreign currency. Some traders find this answer about personal use currency taxation in IRS publications, but it doesn't apply to investing and trading forex. Traders and investors use Section 988 by default.

OTHER INSTRUMENTS

Traders have a bevy of new financial products to choose from, but unfortunately, the IRS is a bit slow to issue tax guidance. It often waits to see how traders use the new instruments, how they report the transactions on tax returns, and how the markets react.

Cryptocurrencies. Selling, exchanging, or using cryptocurrency triggers capital gains and losses for traders. The IRS treats cryptocurrencies as intangible property.

The realization method applies to short-term vs. long-term capital gains and losses. Traders investing in cryptocurrencies and selling, exchanging, or spending some during the year must report a capital gain or loss on each transaction. Tax reporting includes cryptocurrency-to-fiat-currency sales, crypto-to-alt-crypto trades, and purchases of goods or services using crypto.

Some U.S. cryptocurrency exchanges issue a Form 1099-K to accounts with transactions over a certain threshold. Others give a 1099-MISC or 1099-B. The problem for the IRS is that many cryptocurrency transactions on exchanges worldwide are not evident for tax reporting. Cryptocurrency investors should download all crypto transactions into an IRS-compliant crypto accounting program.

Wash sales do not apply to intangible property. Section 475 MTM does not apply to cryptocurrency because it's not a security or a commodity in the eyes of the IRS.

In most cases, crypto traders use the first-in-first-out (FIFO) accounting method. For transactions in intangible property, an investor should use the "specific identification method" that requires some special procedures. Few traders meet those requirements, so they use FIFO. See FIFO vs. Specific Identification in Chapter 4.

TCJA restricted Section 1031 like-kind exchanges to real property starting in 2018. That rules out using like-kind exchange on crypto-to-crypto trades (i.e., Bitcoin for Ethereum). Whether crypto traders could have used Section 1031 before 2018 to defer capital gains taxes is questionable. The IRS mailed tax "education" notices to thousands of crypto traders and released new FAQs about hard forks, airdrops, and other open questions. See the IRS page: Frequently Asked Questions on Virtual Currency Transactions (https://tinyurl.com/virtual-currency).

Volatility ETNs. There are many volatility-based financial products to trade, and tax treatment varies. For example, CBOE Volatility Index (VIX) futures are Section 1256 contracts with lower 60/40 MTM tax rates. The NYSE-traded SVXY is an ETF taxed as a security.

Volatility exchange-traded notes (ETN) are structured as "prepaid forward contracts" or as "debt instruments." Our tax counsel says that an ETN prepaid forward contract is not a security in the eyes of the IRS, whereas ETN debt instruments are.

Sales of ETN prepaid forward contracts use the realization method on sales. Long-term capital gains rates apply if held for 12 months or longer. Because it's not a security, ETN prepaid forward contracts (i.e., VXX) are not subject to wash-sale loss adjustments or Section 475 (if elected). ETN debt instruments (i.e., UGAZ) are securities subject to wash-sale losses and Section 475 (if elected). Check the tax section of the ETN prospectus.

Our tax attorney says there is substantial authority to treat CBOE-listed options on volatility ETNs and volatility ETFs structured as publicly traded partnerships as "non-equity options" with Section 1256 treatment. See our blogs: How To Apply Lower Tax Rates To Volatility Options (https://tinyurl.com/volatility-option and ETNs Have Different Structures With Varying Tax Treatment (https://tinyurl.com/gtt-etns).

In preparing Form 1099-Bs, many brokers use the tax classification determined by exchanges for labeling securities vs. 1256 contracts. Some brokers treat both ETNs as securities on 1099-Bs with wash-sale loss adjustments, even though prepaid forward contracts do not fall in that category. Some brokers treat CBOE-listed options on volatility ETNs and ETF PTPs as securities on Form 1099-Bs, even though they are eligible for Section 1256 treatment. Taxpayers should consider departing from 1099-Bs based on substantial authority positions and explain why in a tax return footnote.

Swap contracts. The Dodd-Frank financial regulation law promised to clear private swap transactions on exchanges to protect the markets from another swap-induced financial meltdown — remember those credit default swaps with insufficient margins? When Congress enacted Dodd-Frank in 2010, traders hoped that clearing on futures exchanges would allow Section 1256 tax treatment. They were wrong: Congress and the IRS immediately communicated that Section 1256 would not apply to swap transactions, and they confirmed ordinary gain or loss treatment. Please read our blog post: Tax Treatment for Swaps Options, https://tinyurl.com/gtt-swaps.

Foreign futures. By default, futures contracts listed on international exchanges are not Section 1256. If the international exchange wants Section 1256 tax treatment, it must obtain an IRS Revenue Ruling. Only a handful of international futures exchanges have Section 1256 treatment: Eurex, LIFFE, ICE Futures Europe, and ICE Futures Canada. Foreign futures are otherwise ST or LT capital gains. (Read our blog Tax Treatment for Foreign Futures https://tinyurl.com/ttfutures to see the list of exchanges with this IRS approval and Updated 2021 US IRC Section 1256 qualified board or exchange list.) Remember, Section 1256 tax treatment uses MTM accounting at year-end. Foreign futures without Section 1256 are reported like securities using the realization method for short- vs. long-term capital gains.

Precious metals. Physical precious metals are a particular class of capital assets called collectibles. If you hold collectibles over 12 months before the sale, you must use the capital gains tax rate applicable to collectibles — capped at 28%. That rate is higher than the top long-term capital gains rate of 20% (2023 and 2024). The short-term capital gains rate applies if you hold collectibles for 12 months or less. Precious metals are not securities, so wash-sale loss adjustments and Section 475 do not apply. Please read our blog post: Tax Treatment for Precious Metals, https://tinyurl.com/gtt-precious.

Chapter 4

Accounting for Trading Gains & Losses

I recommend keeping your accounting for trading gains and losses separate from expenses. A consumer off-the-shelf accounting program is acceptable for keeping track of expenses, non-trading income, home office deductions, and itemized deductions. However, you may need a specialized software program or professional service for trade accounting for securities. Futures gain/loss accounting may not be necessary, as traders generally can rely on the one-page 1099-B with summary reporting using MTM reporting. Forex contract traders can depend on the broker's annual tax reports and should use summary reporting. Spot forex is not a covered security, so Form 1099-B isn't issued.

U.S.-based cryptocurrency exchanges issue Form 1099-K, 1099-Misc., or 1099-B to taxpayers reaching a certain threshold of transactions, and most provide online tax reports. Consider a cryptocurrency trade accounting solution.

THE BIG PICTURE ON WASH SALE LOSSES

Day and swing traders inevitably trigger many wash-sale (WS) loss adjustments amounting to tens or hundreds of thousands of dollars. A WS occurs when you take a loss on a security and repurchase it within 30 days (after or before).

A WS reduces the cost basis on the position sold and adds the loss to the replacement position's cost basis. That defers the WS loss, creating phantom taxable income and capital gains taxes.

It's okay to incur WS losses during the year, but try to avoid delaying them to the following year. Deferring a loss from November to December is acceptable; however, postponing a loss from December 2023 to January 2024 is not.

Learn how to "break the WS chain" at year-end. For example, sell your entire position in security A by Dec. 20, 2023, and don't repurchase it for 30 days, around Jan. 21, 2024. That doesn't provide a WS bridge from the tax year 2023 to 2024. You may deduct the whole year of WS losses in 2023.

When you get your broker-issued Form 1099-B showing massive WS loss adjustments, don't panic. What's critical is the number of WS open at year-end for which you repurchased positions within 30 days in January 2024. For example, suppose the WS loss adjustments column on the 1099-B is $500,000. If you avoided all WS at year-end by refraining from repurchases in January, the cost basis column should be $500,000 greater than your actual purchase price.

The 1099-B calculates taxable income as follows: Proceeds, minus cost basis, plus WS loss adjustments equals net taxable capital gain or loss.

There's a quirky WS rule between taxable and IRA accounts. The WS loss becomes permanent if you take a loss in a taxable account and repurchase the security position within 30 days in an IRA. The IRS does not allow you to add the WS loss adjustment to the IRA cost basis. Yet, the IRS requires a reduction of the cost basis in the taxable account. Avoid this problem with a "do not invest list" in the IRAs vs. what you trade and invest in taxable accounts. This WS rule applies to taxable vs. IRA accounts; an IRA account is not subject to WS losses.

SECURITIES ACCOUNTING IS CHALLENGING

Taxpayers should report proceeds, cost basis, wash-sale loss, other adjustments, holding period, and capital gain/loss for each trade on Form 8949. It's inappropriate to use summary reporting. Details for Form 8949 are on broker-issued Form 1099-Bs. According to Form 8949 instructions, taxpayers without wash sales and other adjustments to cost basis may enter totals from broker 1099-Bs directly on Schedule D and skip filing Form 8949. After all, the IRS gets a copy of the 1099-B with all the details.

Many taxpayers believe that they don't have wash sales when they often have many to report to comply with IRS rules for taxpayers, which differ from rules for brokers.

FORMS 8949 AND 1099-B ISSUES

Per IRS rules for brokers, Form 1099-B reports wash sales for that one brokerage account based on "identical positions." The IRS rules differ for taxpayers, who must calculate wash sales based on "substantially identical positions" across all their accounts, including joint, spouse, and IRAs. In many cases, broker-issued 1099-Bs might report different wash-sale losses than a taxpayer should report on Form 8949. A taxpayer may trigger a wash-sale loss between a taxable and IRA account, but a broker will never account for that on a 1099-B. Sometimes, a broker can report a wash-sale loss deferral at year-end, but the taxpayer may have absorbed the loss in another account, thereby eliminating the problem by year-end.

This problem is still unknown to many taxpayers and tax preparers. Many continue to file a Form 8949, relying solely on broker 1099-B reporting when they should have considered using securities trade accounting software to calculate and report wash-sale loss adjustments based on IRS rules for taxpayers.

Calculating wash sales based on IRS rules for taxpayers leads to unreconciled differences between Form 8949 and 1099-B. Some tax preparers don't want to draw attention to those differences, fearing IRS notices generated from IRS 1099-B automated matching programs. Ironically, the mission of Congress in cost-basis legislation was to "close the tax gap," providing more opportunities for matching 1099-Bs, but it seems to have confused wash sales.

There is one scenario where a taxpayer can confidently rely on a 1099-B: The taxpayer has only one brokerage account, trades equities, and has no activity in nontaxable retirement accounts.

One solution is for traders who qualify for TTS to trade in an entity and elect Section 475 MTM, which is exempt from wash-sale rules. Another solution is to trade Section 1256 contracts. Traders can keep investment accounts with far less wash-sale loss activity on the individual level.

WASH-SALE LOSS RULES

Per IRS Publication 550: "A wash sale occurs when you (a taxpayer) sell or trade stock or securities at a loss and within 30 days before or after the sale you:

- Buy **substantially identical stock or securities**,

- Acquire substantially identical stock or securities in a fully taxable trade,
- Acquire a contract or **option** to buy substantially identical stock or securities, or
- Acquire substantially identical stock for your retirement account **(IRA) or Roth IRA**."

WASH SALES REPORTED ON 1099-B

Broker 1099-Bs report "wash-sale loss disallowed" (box 1g), and it's not uncommon to see an enormous amount for an active securities trader. The 1099-B also reports "proceeds" (box 1d), "cost or other basis" (box 1e), and several other related amounts. For example, $10M proceeds minus $9.9M cost or other basis, plus $150,000 of wash-sale loss disallowed, equals $250,000 of taxable capital gains. Generally, the 1099-B cover page has summary numbers, and supplemental schedules include each securities trade for the previously summarized numbers.

The essential point is that the WS loss disallowed in box 1g is for the entire tax year. However, WS losses deferred at year-end cause phantom income in the current tax year. Many WS losses during the year might fade away by year-end (more on this topic later). Unfortunately, brokers do not report WS losses deferred at year-end, even though taxpayers need that information. If a trader uses trade accounting software, they need the amounts deferred by ticker from one year to the next to continue to track the deferred amount and deduct it in the following year when calculations allow the release of the loss.

For example, two traders can have $1M of WS loss disallowed in box 1g. Trader A doesn't have WS losses at year-end and is not concerned with those adjustments during the year. They sold all open positions by year-end and did not repurchase substantially identical positions in January. Trader B also sold all positions by year-end, but they repurchased trades in January, which triggered $50,000 of WS losses deferred at year-end. Trader B delayed the December WS loss to the subsequent tax year. The 1099-B issued by the brokerage firm will not specify the $50,000 deferred loss. Therefore, the loss will be lumped in the total wash-sale loss adjustment for the entire year.

Traders need ongoing WS loss information throughout the year to prevent this predicament. Some monthly brokerage statements include cost basis amounts for month-end open positions listed on the report; others do not.

Most traders don't realize they have a WS loss problem until they receive 1099-Bs in late February of the subsequent year. That's too late to avoid WS losses.

STRATEGIES TO AVOID WASH-SALE LOSSES ON SECURITIES

Consider keeping a "do not trade" list to avoid permanent wash-sale losses between taxable and IRA accounts.

For example, a trader could trade big-tech stocks in his taxable accounts and ETFs in his IRA accounts. Otherwise, they can never report a wash-sale loss with an IRA, as there is no way to record the loss in the IRA — it's permanent.

Taxpayers can "break the chain" on wash-sale losses at year-end in taxable accounts to avoid deferral. Suppose a trader sells Apple equity at a loss on Dec. 20, 2023. In that case, he shouldn't repurchase Apple equity or Apple equity options until Jan. 21, 2024, avoiding the 30-day window to trigger a wash-sale loss and break the chain.

Wash-sale loss adjustments during the year in taxable accounts can be absorbed if traders sell/buy those open positions before year-end and don't buy/sell them back in 30 days. It means there won't be a wash-sale loss deferral at year-end.

Consider a Section 475 election. Business traders qualifying for TTS are entitled to elect Section 475 mark-to-market (MTM) accounting, which exempts them from wash-sale loss adjustments and the capital-loss limitation. Section 475 business trades use Form 4797 Part II (ordinary gain or loss). Although Section 475 extricates securities traders from the compliance headaches of Form 8949, it does not change their requirement for line-by-line reporting on Form 4797. We recommend trade accounting software to generate Form 4797. Section 475 traders also need that software to calculate the Section 481(a) adjustment. (Learn more about this adjustment in Chapter 2.)

Trade futures. Section 1256 contracts (futures) and ETN prepaid forward contracts, cryptocurrencies, precious metals, and swap contracts are not securities.

For more details, see https://tinyurl.com/wash-sale-loss.

FIFO VS. SPECIFIC IDENTIFICATION ACCOUNTING METHODS

By default, the IRS, brokerage firms, and most trade accounting programs use the First-In-First-Out (FIFO) accounting method for securities. If you sell security A, its cost-basis is the first lot purchased — the first one "out" or sold. FIFO suits most active securities traders.

Another option is called the Specific Identification (SI) accounting method. Assume an investor bought several lots of security A over the year while the stock increased in price. They might prefer SI accounting instead of FIFO to specify a higher cost-basis lot to reduce their short-term capital gains for 2023. SI enables them to hold the older purchased stock for 12 months at a lower cost-basis for a long-term capital gain taxed at a lower rate (up to 20% for 2023 and 2024 vs. the higher ordinary rates).

The IRS requires contemporaneous action for using SI. You must specify the lot to sell before executing the sale, and the broker must confirm those instructions in writing at that same time. You cannot decide to use SI after the sale's settlement date, like when preparing your tax returns. The IRS provides a little leeway to correct communication errors with the broker by allowing a settlement date rather than a trade date.

FIFO is also widely used for cryptocurrencies. While SI is the default accounting method for intangible property, operating SI with cryptocurrencies is challenging.

See the IRS page: FAQ on Virtual Currency Transactions (https://tinyurl.com/virtual-currency). "Q40: How do I identify a specific unit of virtual currency? You may identify a specific unit of virtual currency either by documenting the specific unit's unique digital identifier, such as a private key, public key, and address, or by records showing the transaction information for all units of a specific virtual currency, such as Bitcoin, held in a single account, wallet, or address. This information must show 1) the date and time each unit was acquired, 2) your basis and the fair market value of each unit at the time it was acquired, 3) the date and time each unit was sold, exchanged, or otherwise disposed of, and 4) the fair market value of each unit when sold, exchanged, or disposed of, and the amount of money or the value of property received for each unit."

ACCOUNTING FOR FOREIGN SECURITIES CAN BE CONFUSING

Many traders have trading accounts in foreign countries, and the reporting can be challenging. The tax rules involve an election to keep books in a foreign currency — a qualified business unit (QBU) — which makes accounting easier than converting each trade into U.S. dollars on the day of the transaction. Instead, a taxpayer could use the year's average currency conversion rate. However, if the taxpayer ceases to be a trader, the QBU elective status drops.

SECTION 1256 TRADERS HAVE IT EASIER

Traders probably do not need a trade accounting solution for Section 1256 contracts since broker 1099-Bs are generally accurate. Section 1256 includes U.S. futures, broad-based indexes (stock index futures), options on both, and non-equity options (see Chapter 3).

Summary MTM reporting means taxpayers can enter the "aggregate profit or loss on contracts" from Form 1099-B on Form 6781. MTM is exempt from wash-sale rules since there are no open positions or adjustments to consider at year-end. Broker tax reporting matches taxpayer reporting.

Specific instruments may qualify for Section 1256 treatment, like options on commodity ETFs and CBOE-listed options on volatility ETNs, but the broker may not report it that way. Conversely, the broker may report 1256 treatment (such as on foreign futures), which may not be correct. A good securities accounting program can download all trades, and you can adequately classify Section 1256 contracts vs. securities.

Futures brokers establish separate accounts from securities accounts since the CFTC and NFA regulate futures and the SEC regulates securities. Different regimes for protecting money exist: SIPIC for securities and NFA segregation rules for futures. Separation for regulatory purposes jives nicely with tax reporting.

FOREX TRADERS HAVE IT FAIRLY EASY

Spot forex is not a covered instrument for 1099-B issuance. Online forex brokers provide trade accounting, including a summary of annual forex trading gains or losses. Combine transaction costs, rollover interest (in most cases), and other items into the net trading gain or loss amount reported in a summary fashion. (Read more about forex tax treatment in Chapter 3.)

Section 988 accounting. Most brokers use the realization (cash) method of reporting for realized Section 988 transactions. Few include gain or loss on unrealized positions at year-end. Section 988 doesn't require MTM, but using Section 1256(g) does. If a taxpayer opts out of Section 988 into Section 1256(g), use lower 60/40 MTM tax treatment on major currency pairs. Learn more about Section 1256(g) in Chapter 3.

Rollover transaction reporting isn't always straightforward. Forex brokers often report rollover interest income or expense when generated. It's not a traditional interest expense but a transaction gain or loss element. However, some experts view the "roll open, roll close" method used by some forex brokers as actual interest income or expense.

Most spot forex brokers don't report the flip side of the rollover transaction: The appreciation or depreciation of the string of underlying rollover transactions until those rollover trades are closed out. We think brokers should report rollovers as closed transactions with a replacement trade opened rather than kicking the can down the road on the appreciation or depreciation of the rollover transaction.

KEEP TRACK OF EXPENSES YEAR-ROUND

TTS traders benefit from business expense deductions. Many traders are unsure if they will qualify for TTS until year-end, so they must keep track of all trading and other expenses in their accounting solution throughout the year. They can use a consumer accounting program, solution, or app. At a minimum, traders should keep track of all expenses using a spreadsheet.

TRADING ENTITY

Trading entities should also keep track of additions and withdrawals of capital, purchases of fixed and intangible assets, debt, and profit distributions. An entity tax return includes a balance sheet with all these items, so it is vital to reconcile all asset, liability, and equity items in addition to income and expenses. S-Corps need to account for stock and debt basis.

Chapter 5

Trading Business Expenses

Traders eligible for "trader tax status" (TTS) can deduct reasonable business expenses, whether they have trading gains or losses, saving around $6,000 annually on average. Per the IRS Website, "Section 162(a) allows a deduction for all the ordinary and necessary expenses paid or incurred during the taxable year in carrying on any trade or business."

The 2017 Tax Cuts and Jobs Act (TCJA) suspended "certain miscellaneous itemized deductions subject to the 2% floor," including investment, job, and tax compliance fees and expenses. TCJA did not suspend investment interest (margin interest) or "other itemized deductions."

An active trader can still assess and claim trader tax status (TTS) — business expense treatment — for 2023 and 2024 and even other open tax years (usually up to three years prior via an amended return). The Section 475 MTM (mark-to-market) accounting election is different from claiming trader status, and the TTS trader must elect Section 475 MTM by the April 15 deadline (i.e., April 18, 2023, for 2023, and April 15, 2024, for 2024).

INVESTORS

Investors are stuck with only a few itemized deductions after TCJA suspended investment fees and expenses.

Many investors will choose the 2023 standard deduction of $27,700 for married filing jointly, $13,850 for single/married filing separately, and $20,800 for a head of household. There is an additional standard deduction for age 65 or older or if blind.

For 2024, with an inflation adjustment, the IRS increased the standard deduction to $29,200 for married filing jointly, $14,600 for single/married filing separately, and $21,900 for heads of household.

Investment-interest expenses remain an itemized deduction if they don't exceed net investment income (on Form 4952) and carry over the excess to the following tax year(s).

With TTS, treat margin interest on business positions as a business-interest expense, deductible on Schedule C, or a separate entity business tax return. TCJA introduced a "business interest limitation" Section 163(j) applicable to taxpayers with average annual gross receipts over $25 million. (Gross receipts are trading gains for TTS traders.) See TCJA changes in Chapter 17.

Suppose a taxpayer easily qualifies for TTS, individually or in an entity. Which business expenses are deductible, and which ones are not?

BUSINESS EXPENSES

Business deductions include:

- Tangible personal property like a computer, up to $2,500 per item, providing the taxpayer files a Sec. 1.263(a)-1(f)) safe harbor election with the tax return.
- Section 179 (100%), 100% bonus, or regular depreciation on computers, equipment, furniture, and fixtures (over $2,500 per item).
- Amortization of startup costs (Section 195), organization costs (Section 248), and software.
- Education expenses paid and courses taken after the commencement of the trading business activity.
- Section 195 startup costs may include education expenses within six months of beginning TTS.
- Books/publications, market data, charting services, online and professional services, cloud services, chat rooms, mentors, coaches, supplies, phone, Internet, travel, meals, seminars, conferences, assistants, consultants, office rent, and more.
- Home office expenses for the business use portion of a trader's home (share of rent, mortgage interest, real estate tax, depreciation on home, utilities, repairs, insurance, and all other home costs).
- Margin interest expenses (not limited to investment income).
- Interest expense on trading capital
- Stock-borrow fees and other costs for short sellers.
- Self-created software for automated trading systems.

Business deductions don't include the following:

- Vehicles
- Commissions
- Employee-benefit plan deductions (TTS S-Corps can arrange health insurance and retirement plan contributions in connection with officer compensation)

Vehicles aren't usually deductible because traders don't need a car to visit clients or companies. Mileage for driving to seminars might qualify as travel expenses at the standard mileage rate. Traders must track the miles driven for such travel and the travel dates, destination, and purpose for documentation purposes and to claim the expense deduction.

Commissions are deductible against trading gains and losses; they aren't separately stated business expenses.

Traders may not deduct employee-benefit plan deductions unless they trade in an S-Corp and pay themselves officer's compensation. Employee benefits include health insurance premiums paid during the entity period and retirement plan contributions. See Chapters 7 and 8.

CASH VS. ACCRUAL

A trading business may only elect cash or accrual accounting methods for business expenses. Other rules dictate trading gains and losses, including Section 475 MTM, Section 1256, Section 988, and the various code sections for capital gains and losses.

Most business traders choose the cash method for expenses, meaning expenses are deductible when paid. The accrual method deducts expenses when incurred. Under the cash method, a credit card charged by Dec. 31 or a check dated Dec. 31 is considered a year-end tax cash deduction, provided you place the item in service before year-end.

Here's one case where the accrual method may be better: Suppose a new trader purchases $10,000 of trading training (not classic education) on Dec. 1, 2023. The trader starts classes in December and continues them through March 2024. The trader begins the TTS trading business halfway through the training in January 2024. The cash method classifies the $10,000 as a Section 195 startup cost, with $5,000 deducted in 2024 as "expense allowance" amortization and the balance over 15 years. With the accrual method, the trader will have the same amortization amount ($5,000) on their 2024 tax return. They can deduct the other $5,000 as a post-business-commencement education expense in 2024 because half occurred after business commencement in January. Pre-business education is a nuanced area.

DEPRECIATION ON HARD ASSETS

Some expenses or costs must be capitalized and depreciated (on hard assets) or amortized (on soft or intangible assets) over their "useful life," according to the IRS. Depreciate computers and equipment with various accelerated or straight-line depreciation methods over five years. The same rules apply to furniture and fixtures, but their useful life is seven years. Residential property, including a home office, has a 39-year useful life, and only straight-line depreciation is allowed. For more information on depreciable assets and depreciation methods, see IRS Publication 946: How To Depreciate Property.

When appropriate, taxpayers should skip capitalization and depreciation and use full expensing for "tangible personal property" like a computer, up to $2,500 per item, providing they file a Sec. 1.263(a)-1(f)) safe harbor election with the tax return. In some situations, Section 179 applies, which allows 100% of the cost of the item, even if over $2,500 per item. Section 179 depreciation requires profit from trading and or wages.

TCJA allows "full expensing," or 100% bonus depreciation, for qualified property acquired and placed in service after Sept. 27, 2017, and before Jan. 1, 2023. Beginning with property acquired after Jan. 1, 2023, the percentage of expensing allowed decreases in 20% increments through 2027. In other words, property acquired between Jan. 1 and Dec. 31, 2023, will be expensed at 80%, while property acquired from Jan. 1, 2024 through Dec. 31, 2024, will be expensed at 60%, and so on.

SECTION 179 DEPRECIATION

Certain assets (such as computers, equipment, furniture, and fixtures) qualify for Section 179 depreciation, which allows an immediate 100% write-off per specific IRS rules.

Section 179 depreciation requires business income or wages to offset it; otherwise, it's a carryover item. In that case, regular depreciation may be preferable. Taxpayers can't take Section 179 or bonus depreciation on assets they own before forming their business, so regular depreciation is applied. The assets must be new to the taxpayer, meaning the asset can be purchased used, but it must have been purchased during the tax year to qualify.

TCJA increased the Section 179 limit to $1 million and indexed it for inflation after 2018.

TANGIBLE PERSONAL PROPERTY EXPENSING

Generally, a business must capitalize property for depreciation purposes. The IRS allows expensing under its tangible property regulations for smaller purchases since it's inconvenient to maintain depreciation records on small amounts. The IRS increased the de minimis expensing amount to $2,500 from $500 for 2016 and forward and allowed early adoption to 2015 tax filings.

Under the change, the new $2,500 threshold applies to any item substantiated by an invoice. The purchases can be on one invoice, but it may draw more IRS attention and require more time to break out. Separate invoices are good practical guidance to avoid this issue.

If a business trader purchases a new workstation for $7,500, they should try to break down the purchase into separate items, each under $2,500. For example, they could buy a computer separately from the monitors and other equipment. With all invoices under $2,500, the entire $7,500 can be a current-year business expense without capitalization for fixed assets and related depreciation. That leads to faster expensing, tax benefits, and less compliance work.

STARTUP AND ORGANIZATION EXPENSES

Capitalize startup expenses and amortize them over 15 years (Section 195). The first-year expense allowance is $5,000, whether a taxpayer starts the business toward the beginning or later in the year. Startup expenses are limited to "investigating and inquiring" about a new business. Otherwise, they may be capitalized to the cost of an investment in a new business and not amortized. Organization expenses (Section 248) are like Section 195, and they also have a $5,000 first-year expense allowance with the balance amortized on a straight-line basis over 15 years. Organization costs include attorney and accounting fees for forming a trading entity. Generally, the "lookback" period for startup and organization costs is six months before starting the trading activity.

EDUCATION

Educational expenses incurred after a trading business commences are tax deductible, provided the education maintains or improves the company. Pre-business education expenses, however, are a problem for tax-deduction purposes. Before 2018, education did not qualify as an "investment expense" (Sections 212 and 274(h)(7)). We advise TTS traders to squeeze a reasonable amount of pre-business education expenses into Section 195 startup expenses, which may be appropriate under certain circumstances. Trading education isn't classic secondary school education, and this approach can work. Education must be in the recent past (around six months before active trading begins), and traders should only capitalize a reasonable amount.

C-CORPS DON'T NAVIGATE AROUND TTS

Stay clear of tax promoters promising business deductions for pre-business education using C-Corps and going back more than six months. Those schemes don't work: C-Corps are for business, not pure investing without TTS. A C-Corp may deduct business and ancillary investment expenses, but not just those if it doesn't have a business purpose. The dangerous scheme calls for an LLC (a dual entity) to pay advisory fees to the C-Corp to make a profit and utilize the education expenses dumped into it. One cannot capitalize pre-business education to Section 195 without a business purpose later in the C-Corp. The LLC is an investment company — it does not qualify for TTS — and its fees paid to the C-Corp will pass through as a suspended investment expense on the LLC Schedule K-1 to the owner's tax return. The IRS will view the C-Corp as trading one's own money without TTS and not allow it to use business expense treatment. That's lots of scheming and fees paid to promoters to wind up with no business deduction. In our view, the C-Corp used in this way breaks tax rules and risks back taxes, tax penalties, and interest expenses. Don't fall prey to the snake oil salespeople. (See our blog post How To Avoid IRS Challenge On Your Family Office, https://tinyurl.com/gtt-family.)

AUTOMATED TRADING SYSTEMS

Increasingly, traders are writing computer code for developing automated trading systems. The IRS allows a few different choices for expensing "internal-use software."

Taxpayers who qualify for TTS before incurring software development costs may deduct them like other research expenses in Section 174(a) in the year paid.

Taxpayers not qualifying for TTS before incurring these costs may capitalize them under Section 174(b). This taxpayer has two choices. Once they complete the software, they can wait until they qualify for TTS to amortize (expense) the intangible asset over 60 months. The other option is to wait until the software is in service with the qualification for TTS to amortize the intangible asset over 36 months.

Traders may qualify for TTS using an automated trading system if they write the code or have other significant involvement with its creation and modification. Conversely, a trader using an off-the-shelf automated trading system probably doesn't get credit toward TTS for the volume and frequency of trades made by the software. If the trader does not create the ATS, the related costs are a suspended investment expense. (For additional discussion on this subject, see Chapter 1.)

TRAVEL AND MEALS

Many traders attend seminars and workshops to further their trading education. Many trading seminars are in resorts or fun cities like Las Vegas and New York City. This travel is a business expense, provided the education qualifies as a business expense, as their tax treatment is connected. Travel for classes, seminars, and conferences looks at the underlying tax treatment of that item itself as a non-deductible investment expense (Section 274(h)(7)), Section 195 startup cost, or allowable business expense after business commencement. Deducting a trading seminar trip hinges on previously qualifying for TTS, too. The precedent here is a 2008 IRS revenue ruling that said an investor couldn't deduct travel expenses to and from a real estate investment seminar because the taxpayer didn't qualify for business status before the trip.

Meals with trader colleagues may be tax deductible, but the expenses must be reasonable. Visit www.irs.gov to learn the many IRS rules on travel and meal expenses. The IRS likes to scrutinize meals in tax exams.

Starting in 2018, TCJA disallows a deduction for an activity generally considered entertainment, amusement, or recreation and membership dues for any club organized for business, pleasure, recreation, or other social purposes. The 50% limit on the meals deduction remained and expanded to meals provided through an in-house cafeteria or otherwise on the employer's premises. It's a stretch for stay-at-home TTS traders to deduct in-house meals. The 2020 year-end pandemic relief legislation raised the 50% deduction to 100% for 2021 and 2022 for food or beverages purchased from a restaurant meant for immediate consumption (likely does not include food from grocery stores). Beginning in 2023, the deduction limitation returned to the pre-pandemic 50% limitation.

HOME OFFICE EXPENSES

Since 1999, the home office deduction is no longer a red flag — millions of Americans benefit from this deduction each year. Countless Americans run businesses from home, and the IRS understands this. The income-requirement rule limits the use of this deduction to profitable companies, which appeases IRS concerns about abuse and hobby-loss businesses. Before the IRS liberalized home office deduction rules in 1999, a more stringent requirement was that taxpayers needed to meet clients in their home office. Only administration work is required in a home office; another principal office outside the home office doesn't negate the deduction.

Most traders operate their business from a home office. Some trade from job locations using browser-based trading platforms or apps accessible on work computers, laptops, tablets, and smartphones. They can also qualify for the home office expense deduction in this situation. Home office deductions are very beneficial for profitable business traders.

Unlike other business costs, which require new cash outlays, deducting home office expenses is especially rewarding because you convert fixed personal costs into tax-deductible business expenses.

This same concept applies to many other items such as phones, the Internet, furniture, fixtures, etc. Remember that trading gains are needed to unlock most home office deductions. If a trader has insufficient TTS trading gains, carry over the home office deduction to the following tax years. (In this situation, hopefully, the trader remains in the business and has trading gains in subsequent years to use the carryovers.)

There are several special requirements and rules for the home office deduction. A home office must be exclusively and regularly used for business, meaning children and guests can't use this room. Report "indirect expenses" on Form 8829 and include every expense and cost related to the home: depreciation or rent, utilities, insurance, repairs and maintenance, security, cleaning, lawn care, and more.

Include mortgage interest and real property taxes; this portion doesn't require income. The non-business amount of mortgage interest and real property taxes are considered itemized deductions on Schedule A. Real property taxes on Schedule A are part of TCJA's SALT limitation, but the home office portion or real property tax is not subject to the SALT limit.

To calculate the home office deduction, take the home office's square footage (and all related business areas such as storage, hallways, and bathrooms) and divide it by the total home square footage (10-15% is customary). Alternatively, taxpayers can do the apportionment based on the room's method. Form 8829 multiplies the home office percentage by the indirect expenses. If a trader files a partnership return, deduct home office expenses as unreimbursed partnership expenses (UPE) on Schedule E. We prefer an accountable reimbursement plan in S-Corps, which a TTS trader must "use or lose" before year-end.

Including home depreciation doesn't reduce the gain exclusion allowed under Section 121 if the taxpayer sells the principal residence in later years. When a taxpayer sells their main residence, recapture a portion of depreciation, whether or not you take the depreciation expense. The required recapture amount is what is "allowed or allowable" (an IRS phrase), meaning traders should depreciate their home offices on Form 8829 because the IRS will treat it as if they did anyway. Suppose the taxpayer has a gain on the sale of a residence containing a home office. In that case, the recapture (meaning to report a portion as taxable) of home office depreciation means there was only a temporary tax break for the depreciation portion. That is still very helpful.

The net loss is not deductible if a taxpayer sells the residence at a loss. However, the recapture of depreciation income may not surpass the loss amount, meaning there is no taxable income from depreciation recapture to report on the tax return.

Chapter 6 explains how to execute the home office deduction.

Starting in 2018, Schedule A itemized deductions for any combination of state and local income taxes, sales taxes, real property taxes, and personal property taxes (SALT) were capped by TCJA at $10,000 for all filers (except married filing separately, which has a $5,000 cap). TCJA also changed itemized deduction limits on mortgage interest expenses and casualty losses.

A HYBRID CASE

Some traders have both business trading expenses and suspended investment expenses. Since they aren't part of the trading business, investment fees and costs associated with a trader's outside-managed investment account or an account using an outside-developed automated trading system get suspended. Traders may have interest expense on core investment positions and business margin interest on business trading. Be careful to apportion these expenses properly. A trader might use margin lending on investment positions as capital for trading positions, and that should qualify as business interest.

NON-ACTIVE SPOUSES

Non-active spouses/partners in an LLC filing a TTS partnership or S-Corp tax return must use investment-interest expense treatment. Still, a TTS entity's active spouse/partner is entitled to business interest treatment. Non-active spouses/partners get the rest of TTS business expense treatment and use of Section 475 if duly elected. Section 469 passive-activity loss rules don't apply to a trading business.

Spouses/partners are "active" if they trade or perform administrative duties. If a spouse is not active, and if margin interest is significant, a taxpayer may want to give the spouse only 1-10% interest rather than 50% interest in the pass-through entity to limit the interest treated as an investment interest expense. However, taxpayers living in a community property state may want to use 50/50 ownership.

If a spouse is active in the TTS business, consider including the spouse in S-Corp compensation and employee benefits. Don't overpay a spouse, which is a related party transaction.

RETIREMENT PLAN TRADING

Suppose traders conduct business trading and retirement plan trading simultaneously. In that case, we generally consider the latter ancillary to the trading business and don't believe it is necessary to apportion expenses away from it. If the retirement plan trading dwarfs the trading business in size and the trading business is immaterial to the level of costs — in other words, if the expenses lead to a significant business loss — it may be appropriate to apportion some fees to the retirement plan. (More on retirement account trading and reimbursement of investment expenses in Chapter 8.)

Chapter 6

Trader Tax Return Reporting Strategies

The IRS uses multiple tax forms for trading businesses eligible for trader tax status (TTS). It can be confusing to taxpayers, accountants, and the IRS. Traders enter gains and losses, portfolio income, and business expenses in various tax forms. Which tax form or schedule should a forex trader use? It depends on their circumstances. Which form is correct for securities traders using the Section 475 MTM method? Can trading gains be reported directly on Schedule C? The different reporting strategies for the various types of traders make tax time not so cut and dry.

SOLE PROPRIETOR TRADING BUSINESS

Most sole proprietorship businesses report revenue, cost of goods sold, and expenses on Schedule C. However, business traders qualifying for TTS report only trading business expenses on Schedule C. Trading gains and losses are reported in other tax forms, depending on the situation. They can consolidate trading gains, losses, and business expenses on an entity tax return — a partnership Form 1065 or S-Corp Form 1120-S.

Sales of securities for each trade (no summary reporting) are reported on Form 8949, which feeds into Schedule D (cash method) with capital losses limited to $3,000 per year against ordinary income (the rest is a capital loss carryover). Capital losses are unlimited against capital gains. (We cover Form 8949 in Chapter 4.)

TTS traders who elect and use Section 475 MTM on securities report each securities trade on Form 4797 Part II. MTM means open securities trades are marked-to-market at year-end prices. Traders still report sales of segregated investments in securities (without MTM) on Form 8949 and Schedule D. Form 4797 Part II receives ordinary gain or loss treatment, avoiding the capital loss limitation and wash-sale loss rules. Net operating loss (NOL) calculations include Form 4797 losses that cause negative taxable income. The 20% qualified business income (QBI) deduction includes Section 475 gains and excludes capital gains and portfolio income.

Section 1256 contract traders (i.e., futures) should use Form 6781 (but if they elected Section 475 for commodities/futures, they should report them on Form 4797). Section 1256 traders don't use Form 8949 — they rely on a one-page Form 1099-B showing their net trading gain or loss ("aggregate profit or loss on contracts"). The futures gain loss amount is shown in summary format on Form 6781 Part I.

If the trader has a significant Section 1256 loss, they should consider carrying back the loss three tax years but only apply it against Section 1256 gains in those years. To make this election, check box D labeled "Net section 1256 contracts loss election" on the top of Form 6781 filed on a timely basis.

Spot forex traders with Section 988 ordinary gains or losses who don't qualify for TTS should use line 8(z) (other income or loss) on 2023 Schedule 1 (Form 1040). TTS traders should use Form 4797, Part II, ordinary gain or loss. What's the difference? Form 4797 Part II losses contribute to NOL carryforwards against any income, whereas Form 1040's "other losses" do not. With a capital gains election to opt out of Section 988, use Form 8949 for minor currencies and Form 6781 for major currency pairs (under Section 1256(g). Forex uses summary reporting. (We cover forex tax treatment in Chapter 3 and forex accounting treatment in Chapter 4.)

For sales of cryptocurrencies, use Form 8949, but not wash sales or Section 475 MTM.

SCHEDULE C RED FLAG ISSUES

Sole-proprietor TTS traders report business expenses on Schedule C and trading income/loss and portfolio-related income on other tax forms, which may confuse the IRS. Because of this, the IRS may automatically view a trading business's Schedule C as unprofitable even if it has significant net trading gains on other forms and is profitable after expenses. To mitigate this red flag, we advocate a particular strategy to transfer a portion of business trading gains to Schedule C to "zero it out" if possible. Needing an individual transfer strategy is one reason we recommend an entity where a trader doesn't need an income transfer.

TRANSFER TRADING GAINS TO SCHEDULE C

Sometimes, a good strategy for sole proprietorship business traders is to transfer some business trading gains from Form 4797, Form 8949 or Form 6781 to Schedule C, using the "Other Income" line, to zero the expenses but not show a net profit. Showing a profit could cause the IRS to inquire about self-employment (SE) tax, from which trading gains are exempt. (Traders who are full members of a futures or options exchange with dealer rights are an exception here; they have self-employment income under Section 1402(i) on their exchange-generated trading gains reported on Form 6781.)

This unique income-transfer strategy can also unlock the home office and Section 179 (100%) depreciation deductions; both require income. While Section 179 depreciation can look to wage income outside the business, most home office deductions can only look to business income. Tax forms or form instructions do not include this transfer strategy. It's our suggested practice designed to deal with insufficient tax forms for sole-proprietorship trading businesses, and you should explain it in tax-return footnotes. It also allows Schedule C losses in states like New Jersey that don't allow losses.

An alternative strategy: Report gains from trading (from Form 4797, Form 8949, and Form 6781) on Line 8 of the home office Form 8829. It's an alternative way to provide the necessary income required to generate a home office deduction, but it doesn't fix the red flag of a Schedule C loss, as with the income-transfer strategy.

INCLUDE FOOTNOTES

We recommend that business traders include tax-return footnotes explaining trader tax law and benefits, why and how they qualify for TTS, whether they elected Section 475 MTM or opted out of Section 988, segregation of investments, and other tax treatment, such as the income-transfer strategy. If the taxpayer is a part-time trader, they should explain how they allocate time between different activities and trading. Footnotes help address any questions the IRS may have about TTS qualification and the various aspects of reporting on the return before asking the taxpayer.

SEPARATE ENTITIES MIGHT BE BETTER

Partnership and S-Corp trading business tax returns show trading gains, losses, and business expenses on one set of forms, plus the IRS won't see the taxpayer's other activities on the same return as the trading activity. That looks better.

Submit Form 1065 for a general partnership or multi-member LLC choosing partnership treatment. Submit Form 1120S for an S-corporation. Forms 1065 and 1120S issue Schedule K-1s to the owners, so taxes are paid at the owner level rather than the entity level, thereby avoiding double taxation. Form 1040 Schedule E shows a summary of ordinary income or loss (primarily business expenses) rather than in detail on Schedule C (hence less IRS attention). Section 179 is broken out separately on Schedule E, along with unreimbursed partnership expenses (UPE), including home office expenses.

Under the "trading rule" exception in Section 469 passive-activity loss rules, trading business entities are considered "active" rather than "passive-loss" activities, so losses are allowed in full on Form 1040 Schedule E in the non-passive income column.

Portfolio income (interest and dividends) is stated separately on the partnership or S-Corp Schedule K-1s and passed through to the individual owner's Schedule B. Capital gains and losses pass through to Schedule D in summary form. A pass-through entity draws less IRS attention than a detailed Schedule C filing. Net taxes don't change; pay them on the individual level. Pass-through entities file Form 8949 or Form 4797 at the entity level. Schedule K-1 line one, "ordinary business income (loss)," consolidates Form 4797 ordinary income or loss with business expenses, and it's a net income amount if trading gains exceed business expenses. That looks better than a sole proprietor trader with expenses only on Schedule C, and trading income reported on many other forms.

TTS S-Corps provides opportunities for deducting retirement plan contributions and health insurance premiums, two breaks sole-proprietor traders and partnership traders can't use unless they have earned income. (Learn more about entities in Chapter 7.)

QBI on Schedule K-1s. Per TCJA, the 2023 partnership and S-Corp Schedule K-1s report QBI (Section 199A) income, wages, property factors, and whether the business is a specified service trade or business (SSTB). A sole proprietor using Section 475 is also eligible for the QBI deduction. Look to TTS trading gains on Form 4797 Part II, less Schedule C TTS expenses. QBI excludes capital gains and portfolio income.

TAX TREATMENT ELECTIONS

Tax treatment elections can be confusing because the Section 475 MTM and Section 988 elections don't have tax forms. New taxpayers — such as a newly formed entity — file Section 475 MTM elections internally within 75 days of inception, but existing taxpayers file an election statement by the due date of the prior year's tax return or extension with the IRS and perfect it later with a Form 3115 filing by the tax return deadline. (See Chapter 2 for details.) The Section 988 capital gains election is filed internally on a contemporaneous basis. (Read about forex tax treatment in Chapter 3.)

FILING AS AN INVESTOR

If a taxpayer is filing as an investor, they should report trading gains and losses, as explained earlier. The taxpayer can't elect and use Section 475 MTM with Form 4797 ordinary gain or loss treatment, as that election requires TTS.

Report investment interest expense (margin interest) on Form 4952. It's limited to net investment income. The excess is a carryover to the subsequent tax year(s). Take the deduction on Schedule A as an itemized deduction. It's also deductible on Form 8960 for net investment tax. (See Obamacare net investment tax in Chapter 15.)

The TCJA SALT cap of $10,000 and suspension of all miscellaneous itemized deductions, including investment fees and expenses, means most investors will receive little to no tax reduction from investing-related costs paid.

Many states limit or do not allow itemized deductions. Business expense treatment with TTS is much better.

REPORTING LARGE TRADING LOSSES ON FORM 8886

Traders with significant trading losses may have to file Form 8886 (Reportable Transaction Disclosure Statement). The instructions mention losses of $2 million in any single tax year ($50,000 if the losses are from certain foreign currency transactions) or $4 million in any combination of tax years. If the forex loss is ordinary under Section 988, the $50,000 rule applies; however, if the forex transactions have capital gains and loss treatment, the $2 million limitation may apply.

File 8886 when due and include a simple explanation. These are not tax shelters; if the IRS sends a tax notice, it should be simple to reply and closeout. Although the taxpayer doesn't need to attach a forex statement from the broker, they may want to so the IRS sees the loss is actual.

FOREIGN ACCOUNTS, INCOME, ASSETS

Foreign bank, brokerage, investment, and other types of accounts — including retirement and insurance in some cases — must be reported annually on FinCEN Form 114. The filing threshold is $10,000 for all foreign accounts combined. Beginning in 2011, the IRS expanded its international compliance with tax form 8938 (Statement of Specified Foreign Financial Assets).

In recent years, the IRS busted thousands of taxpayers for not filing Foreign Bank Account Reports (FBARs) and hiding unreported income offshore. Taxpayers might not even realize they need to file an FBAR. If any of our readers have any connection with foreign matters, it's important to read Chapter 14.

Current rules do not require FBAR reports to include foreign-held cryptocurrencies, although that might change. See https://tinyurl.com/fin-cen.

TAX EXTENSIONS AND TAX PAYMENTS ARE DUE

The 2023 income tax returns for individuals are due by April 15, 2024 — however, most active traders aren't ready to file a complete tax return by then. Some brokers issue corrected 1099-Bs right up to the deadline and often after the filing deadline. Many partnerships and S-Corps file extensions by March 15, 2024, and don't issue final Schedule K-1s to investors until after April 15.

Traders don't have to rush to complete their tax returns by April 15. They can use a simple one-page automatic extension and pay taxes owed to the IRS and state.

Traders can request an automatic six-month extension to file individual federal and state income tax returns until Oct. 15, 2024. The 2023 Form 4868 instructions indicate how easy it is to get this automatic extension — no reason is required. It's an extension to file a complete tax return, not an extension to pay taxes owed. The taxpayer should estimate and report what they think they owe for 2023 based on the tax information received.

We suggest taxpayers learn how the IRS and states assess late-filing and late-payment penalties so they can avoid or reduce them. If taxpayers cannot pay the taxes owed, they should estimate the balance due by April 15 and report it on the extension. Be sure to at least file the automatic extension on time to avoid the late-filing penalties, which are much higher than the late-payment penalty. See the 2023 Form 4868, page two, for an explanation of how to calculate these penalties. Another resource: Tax Extensions: 12 Tips To Save You Money (https://tinyurl.com/2xya2fzd).

Some traders made massive trading gains in 2023. Some used the estimated tax payment "safe harbor" exception to cover their 2023 tax liability with the fourth quarter (Q4) 2023 estimated tax payment made by Jan. 16, 2024. They plan to pay the balance of taxes owed by April 15, 2024, and should consider setting aside and protecting those funds. Some will risk their tax funds in the markets. Taxpayers should be careful because losing the funds will cause significant trouble later in the year.

See Traders Should Focus On Q4 Estimated Taxes Due Jan. 16 (https://tinyurl.com/yeys4fh6).

SALT CAP WORKAROUND

TCJA capped state and local income, sales, and property taxes (SALT) at $10,000 per year ($5,000 for married filing separately) and did not index it for inflation. About 30 states enacted SALT cap workaround laws. Search "(Your state) SALT cap workaround" to learn the details for your state. Most states follow a blueprint approved by the IRS.

Generally, you should elect to make a "pass-through entity" (PTE) payment on a partnership or S-Corp tax return filed by your business. It doesn't work with a sole proprietorship filing a Schedule C. PTE is a business expense deduction shown on the state K-1 like a withholding credit. Most states credit the individual's state income tax liability with the PTE amount. Essentially, you convert a non-deductible SALT itemized deduction (over the cap) into a business expense deduction from gross income. Act well before year-end; otherwise, you might delay the benefit to next year. Learn the rules of your state. (See Chapter 19.)

S-CORP ENTITY RETURNS

See About Form 7203, S Corporation Shareholder Stock and Debt Basis Limitations (www.irs.gov/forms-pubs/about-form-7203).

See Chapter 9 on Tax Planning for payroll tax compliance tips for TTS S-Corps to arrange employee benefits, including health insurance deduction and maximizing a Solo 401(k) retirement plan.

Chapter 7

Entity Solutions

Most traders eligible for trader tax status (TTS) begin as sole proprietors (unincorporated businesses). They use a Schedule C as part of their tax return to deduct business expenses. TTS traders can elect Section 475 MTM for 2024 by April 15, 2024, to avoid wash sales losses and the $3,000 capital loss limitation. Section 475 gains are also eligible for the qualified business income (QBI) deduction. We covered sole proprietors in earlier chapters.

If the activity in the entity qualifies for TTS, a pass-through entity, including a partnership or S-corp, can offer several additional tax-saving strategies.

An S-Corp can arrange employee benefits, including deductions for health insurance and retirement plan contributions. Sole proprietorships and partnerships cannot provide employee benefits for owners.

In about 30 states, S-Corps and partnerships can do a SALT cap workaround to convert non-deductible state and local taxes (SALT) into business expenses.

S-Corps and partnerships can ring-fence (segregate) TTS with Section 475 on the entity level versus investments held on the individual level, averting IRS confusion. Hold Apple stock as a personal investment and safely trade Apple options with 475 MTM on the entity without the IRS trying to apply MTM to the investment in Apple.

An entity return consolidates trading activity on a pass-through tax return (partnership Form 1065 or S-Corp 1120S), making life easier for taxpayers, accountants, and the IRS.

Newly formed entities help traders elect Section 475 MTM (ordinary-loss treatment) later in the tax year — within 75 days of inception — if they missed the individual MTM election deadline on April 15, 2024, for the 2024 tax year. It's more convenient for a new entity to adopt Section 475 MTM internally from inception, as opposed to an existing taxpayer who must prepare and file Form 3115 after filing an external election with the IRS. It's also easier for an entity to exit TTS and Section 475 MTM than for a sole proprietor.

Prior capital-loss carryovers on the individual level aren't lost if you form a pass-through entity; these still carry over on Schedule D. The new entity can pass through capital gains if the taxpayer opts to use up individual capital loss carryovers with entity gains by skipping the entity Section 475 MTM election. Then, the entity can elect Section 475 MTM in a subsequent tax year.

There are costs for tax compliance (a separate entity tax return is required), payroll compliance for S-Corps, and minimum taxes in some states. An entity is more formal than a sole proprietorship.

Before forming an entity in your resident state, be confident you'll be eligible for TTS. Try to estimate the benefits versus the costs before creating an entity to be sure it makes sense.

See the article, Choice of Entity for Traders Eligible for TTS (https://tinyurl.com/entitychart).

PASS-THROUGH ENTITIES

We recommend pass-through entities for some traders. A pass-through entity means the entity is a tax filer, but it's not a taxpayer. The owners are the taxpayers, most often on their individual tax returns. Taxpayers should consider marriage, state residence, and state tax rules, including annual reports, minimum taxes, franchise taxes, and more when setting up an entity. Report all entity trading gains, losses, and expenses on the entity tax return and issue a Schedule K-1 to each owner for their respective share. Amounts reported on Schedule K-1 retain their character. For example, the entity can pass through capital gains to utilize capital loss carryovers. Or the entity can pass through Section 475 MTM ordinary gains or losses.

S-CORP UNLOCKS EMPLOYEE BENEFITS

A partnership return is the default treatment for a spousal multi-member Limited Liability Company (LLC). The default tax treatment for a single-member LLC (SMLLC), also known as a "disregarded entity" or a "tax nothing" in the eyes of the IRS, is a Schedule C. Therefore, an SMLLC that qualifies for TTS is back to filing a Schedule C, which a business trader tries to avoid.

A new multi-member LLC and an SMLLC can elect S-Corp tax treatment within 75 days of inception. Existing entities must elect by March 15 of the current tax year. TTS traders should consider an S-Corp election (by filing Form 2553) if they want health insurance and retirement plan contributions. These employee benefits require earned income. Earned income is officer compensation in an S-Corp. Most states accept the federal S-Corp election.

C-Corps may also elect S-Corp status.

S-Corps also provides ring-fencing and SALT cap workaround solutions.

LLC TAXED AS A PARTNERSHIP

A TTS trader can organize a spousal-member LLC and file as a partnership. Only one spouse needs to be an active trader. LLC/partnerships file a Form 1065 partnership tax return and issue Schedule K-1s to owners. Like S-Corporations, LLCs/partnerships must qualify for TTS; otherwise, they are investment companies.

With TTS, report business expenses on page 1 of 1065. List net 475 income or loss, less TTS expenses, on line one of the Schedule K-1 "ordinary business income (loss)." Use separate K-1 line items for portfolio income, including capital gains and losses, interest, and dividends.

The owner reports Schedule K-1 ordinary business income (loss) on Form 1040 Schedule E in the active column. It's not a passive activity in Section 469 under the "trading rule" exception. However, losses are limited to "basis" (your net investment in the partnership). (Sole proprietor TTS traders also need a basis for deducting losses.)

Report capital gains/losses and portfolio income separately on 1040 — schedule B for interest and dividend income and Schedule D for capital gains and losses from partnerships.

If the partnership agreement provides for it, the partner can deduct "unreimbursed partnership expenses," including home office expenses, on Schedule E, page 2. (It's more formal with an S-Corp.)

An LLC/partnership provides a ring-fencing solution and the SALT cap workaround strategy. It cannot generate earned income for the health and retirement plan deductions; you need an S-Corp for employee benefits.

SALT CAP WORKAROUND

TCJA capped state and local income, sales, and property taxes (SALT) at $10,000 per year ($5,000 for married filing separately) and did not index it for inflation. About 30 states enacted SALT cap workaround laws. Search "(Your state) SALT cap workaround" to learn the details for your state. Most states follow a blueprint approved by the IRS. It doesn't work with a sole proprietorship filing a Schedule C.

Generally, elect to make a "pass-through entity" (PTE) payment on a partnership or S-Corp tax return filed by your business. The procedure for making the election varies by state, and each state has different deadlines for payments and elections, so be sure to read the rules that apply to your state early. PTE is a business expense deduction on the Federal K-1 and has the effect of a state withholding credit on the individual state return. Essentially, you convert a non-deductible SALT itemized deduction (over the cap) into a business expense deduction from gross income for Federal purposes. Act well before year-end; otherwise, you might delay the benefit of the tax expense deduction to next year (the year the payment is made is the year the deduction is taken for cash basis taxpayers).

RING-FENCE TRADING FROM INVESTING

Suppose you have or plan to have long-term investments in securities that you also want to trade equity or equity options. In that case, you might need a ring-fencing solution to segregate trading using Section 475 from investments. If you combine investing and trading in the same account or have separate individual accounts, the IRS could look at the investments to challenge TTS and apply Section 475 MTM on investments, which is not what a trader wants. Lack of segregation can undermine eligibility for TTS and cause misapplication of Section 475 mark-to-market (MTM) accounting on your investments. That can ruin the deferral of capital gains and prevent long-term capital gains treatment on those positions.

With an entity, you can fully segregate TTS/475 from investments. (See more about segregation problems in Chapter 1 on TTS and Chapter 2 in Section 475 MTM.

AVOID WASH SALE LOSSES

If you trade substantially identical positions between taxable accounts and IRAs, it could trigger losses for permanent wash sale loss adjustments (WS). Brokers don't recognize this problem on 1099-Bs; the IRS permits them to view WS narrowly.

Take a loss on X in a taxable account and repurchase X within 30 days before or after in an IRA, and it's a permanent WS loss. There is no way to record the WS cost basis adjustments in the IRAs; hence, it's permanent. Conversely, with WS in taxable accounts, you defer the loss to the replacement position, which the broker does on the 1099-B.

There are three ways to avoid these IRA-generated WS. Use a do not trade or invest list to prevent overlap, elect 475 on trades, or use a ring-fencing entity solution. If you only trade an IRA account, there is no WS; it's only a problem between taxable vs. IRS accounts with overlap.

A FEW STATES TAX S-CORPS

An S-Corp is tax-free on the entity level for federal tax purposes, and some states have only small minimum taxes or annual report fees. However, a few state jurisdictions impose higher taxes: On S-Corp net income, Illinois has a 1.5% replacement tax, California has a 1.5% franchise tax, and New York City has an 8.85% general corporate tax.

Illinois replacement tax: S-Corps and partnerships operating in Illinois are liable for the replacement tax of 1.5% on net income. However, an "investment partnership" is exempt from filing an IL Form 1065 partnership tax return. (See Illinois Income Tax Act Section 1501(a)(11.5).) The investment partnership exception does not apply to an S-Corp. If the trading company files an S-Corp Form 1120-S federal tax return, it must also file an IL Form 1120-ST (Small Business Corporation Replacement Tax Return) and pay the replacement tax. Consider increasing officer compensation to reduce this tax or use a dual-entity structure such as a trading partnership and S-Corp management company.

California franchise tax: S-Corps operating in California are liable for the state's franchise tax of 1.5% on net income. The minimum franchise tax is $800 annually, even in a short year; $800 divided by 1.5% equals $53,333. That means an S-Corp owes franchise tax above the $800 minimum tax after net income exceeds $53,333. Deduct officer compensation and employee benefit plans in calculating net income. General partnerships are not liable for an $800 minimum tax, but LLCs are. Only the S-Corp owes 1.5% franchise tax.

Traders may avoid or reduce the California franchise tax using a dual-entity solution: A general partnership trading company and an S-Corp management company. Two entities are difficult and costly to administer. But if you expect significant trading gains and are not committed to maximizing the retirement plan described in the following paragraph, consider dual entities.

Alternatively, traders can use one entity: an S-Corp trading company. The trader should plan to maximize the Solo 401(k) retirement plan contribution and increase officer compensation to reduce franchise tax. Higher wages pay a 2.9% Medicare tax on earned income, plus a 0.9% surtax if over the Obamacare AGI threshold. Medicare on earned income replaces ACA's net investment tax (NIT, 3.8% Medicare surtax) on net investment income if over the NIT AGI threshold. Increasing officer compensation above the amount required for maximizing a Solo 401(k) profit-sharing plan ($43,500 for 2023) requires wages of $174,000. It does not add to the Social Security (FICA) tax since the Social Security base amount is $160,200 for 2023 and $168,600 for 2024.

If a California LLC does not file as an S-Corp or C-Corp, there is an LLC fee based on gross income: $0 if gross income is under $250,000, $900 if under $500,000, $2,500 if under $1 million, $6,000 if under $5 million, $11,790 if over $5 million. Gross income includes net trading gains.

CA also adopted a SALT cap workaround solution.

New York City general corporation tax: New York taxpayers can have an S-Corp for federal and state purposes, but New York City does not acknowledge pass-through S-Corps. NYC assesses a general corporation tax (GCT) on S-Corps of 8.85% times the net income allocated to NYC. Taxpayers can reduce net income with deductions for officer compensation, health insurance, and retirement plans. However, there is an alternative tax: "8.85% of 15% of net income plus the amount of salaries or other compensation paid to any person, including an officer, who at any time during the taxable year owned more than five percent of the taxpayer's issued capital stock," according to NYC CGT Tax Rates.

A dual-entity solution might be better: A general partnership is exempt from NYC's 4% unincorporated business tax (UBT), providing it only has trading income and not advisory fees. The second entity is an S-Corp management company for health insurance and retirement plan deductions. It reduces NYC GCT, but the two companies are more complex and expensive.

GROSS RECEIPTS TAXES

Some state and local governments subject pass-through entities to franchise or business income taxes based on gross receipts, gross margin, or net income. That trend may be growing with states hungry for new revenue streams. However, traders usually have an exemption from these taxes.

The essential point is that trading or investing in financial instruments is buying and selling "capital assets" for capital gains and losses (Section 1221). It's different for "dealers" who hold securities in their inventory as ordinary income property. Dealers have customers and gross receipts from a business, but traders do not.

TTS unlocks business expense treatment; it does not generate "business income." A TTS trader making a Section 475 election generates ordinary income and losses from selling capital assets.

Here are some examples.

Illinois has an exemption for "investment partnerships," but not S-Corps.

Tennessee has a FONCE exemption from its 6% excise tax on S-Corps, and a family trading company qualifies (https://tinyurl.com/tn-taxes).

Nevada exempts trader pass-through entities as "passive entities" from its Commerce Tax (https://tinyurl.com/nv-taxes).

Washington state exempts traders from the Business & Occupancy Tax on pass-through entities (https://tinyurl.com/wa-taxes).

IN-STATE VS. OUT-OF-STATE ENTITIES

Traders can form an entity in a tax-free state like Delaware, but their home state probably requires "foreign entity" registration if it operates there. Setting up a mail forwarding service in a tax-free state does not achieve tax nexus, whereas conducting a trading business from your resident state does.

A pass-through entity in or out of state reports Schedule K-1 income and loss on federal and state individual income tax returns. Don't try to avoid state entity-level taxation. For example, a Delaware LLC/partnership trader who lives, works, and trades in California may incur California's $800 minimum tax and potential LLC fees, plus interest and penalties.

ENTITY TAX RETURNS

S-Corporation tax return: Trading in an S-Corp tax structure means there is no need for a management company. The S-Corp is the best and most straightforward solution if there is no or nominal tax on S-Corps in your state, which is generally the case.

Plan to have officer compensation covering reimbursement of officer/owner health insurance premiums, even when there are trading losses (although profits look better to the IRS). Computing health insurance deduction for officers/owners is a little complicated: Add health insurance premiums paid by the entity or individually during the entity period to wages in box one on the officer/owner's W-2. The health insurance amount in wages is not subject to payroll taxes, so omit this amount from Social Security wages in box three and Medicare wages in box 5. The officer deducts health insurance premiums on their tax return as an adjusted gross income (AGI) deduction. Deduct non-owner employees' health insurance directly on the S-Corp tax return as "insurance expense."

Traders with sufficient trading profits by Q4 may consider establishing a retirement plan before year-end. For a Solo 401(k) defined contribution plan, start with the 100% deductible elective deferral (ED; $22,500 for 2023 and $23,000 for 2024) and pay it through payroll reported on the annual W-2. Taxpayers 50 or older have a catch-up provision for an additional $7,500 for 2023 and 2024. Add the ED to Social Security and Medicare wages on the W-2 but not taxable wages in box 1, as that is where the tax benefit (deduction) is. The gross wage ED component is subject to payroll taxes, and the S-Corp tax return has a deduction for gross wages.

Traders with significant trading gains may consider increasing payroll in December for a performance-based bonus to unlock a 25% Solo 401(k) profit-sharing retirement plan contribution that you don't have to pay until the due date of the tax return (including extensions by Sept. 15). The maximum Solo 401(k) profit-sharing plan amount is $43,500 for 2023 and $46,000 for 2024. The S-Corp tax return deducts the profit-sharing plan contribution. (For details about retirement plans, limits, and savings, see Chapter 8.)

Partnership tax return: If you trade in a spousal-member LLC filing a partnership return, achieving targeted SEI for health insurance and retirement plan AGI deductions is difficult because a partnership passes through negative SEI, whereas an S-Corp does not. Traders may consider an S-Corp election by March 15, 2024, to add these employee benefit deductions for 2024.

For traders who don't need health and retirement plan deductions, the partnership tax structure works fine for TTS, Section 475 MTM, segregation, and a SALT cap workaround.

Ex-employer-provided health insurance, including Cobra, is not deductible. If the trader's spouse has health insurance available for the family from their employer, then the IRS does not permit a self-employed health insurance deduction.

S-CORP PAYROLL TAX COMPLIANCE

Payroll is not a big deal for a TTS trading S-Corp with married or single ownership.

A payroll service includes quarterly payroll tax returns (Form 941), annual payroll tax returns (Form 940), state payroll tax returns, and federal unemployment insurance with an FUI tax of under $50 for the owner/trader. The trader/owner is exempt from state unemployment insurance and workers' compensation in most states.

A trader can withhold taxes from payroll in December and have them attributed to being made throughout the year. Take advantage of this tax loophole to reduce quarterly estimated tax payments during the year. Benefit from hindsight and use of the cash flow.

Plan to execute payroll for the health insurance premium deduction at a minimum, as that does not trigger payroll taxes. Once a business starts payroll, the IRS and state expect quarterly payroll tax returns, even if there is no payroll during a quarter. The payroll vendor handles these filings.

Set the wages based on the desired employee benefits. A TTS S-Corp does not require "reasonable compensation" since the underlying income is unearned.

YEAR-END ENTITY PLANNING

There are significant tax matters to implement with entities before year-end. For example, S-Corps should execute payroll before year-end. You must establish a Solo 401(k) defined contribution plan or defined benefit retirement plan before year-end. S-Corps must reimburse employee business expenses before year-end. (Read about year-end planning in Chapter 9.)

20% DEDUCTION ON QUALIFIED BUSINESS INCOME

In 2018, TCJA introduced a 20% qualified business income deduction (QBI). In a simple scenario, on a QBI of $100,000, the owner might be able to deduct $20,000. That's a tax deduction without spending any money.

Trading is a "specified service trade or business" (SSTB), which means an income cap applies. If your taxable income is over that cap, there is no QBI deduction. QBI includes Section 475 ordinary income, less TTS expenses, and excludes capital gains, portfolio income, and forex trading income.

Taxpayers might be able to increase the QBI deduction with thoughtful year-end planning. Suppose taxable income falls within the phase-out range for an SSTB. You might need higher S-Corp wages (including officer compensation) to avoid a W-2 wage limitation on the QBI deduction.

The taxable income (TI) cap is $464,200/$232,100 (married/other taxpayers) for 2023 and $483,900/$241,950 (married/other taxpayers) for 2024. The phase-out range below the cap is $100,000/$50,000 (married/other taxpayers), in which the QBI deduction phases out for SSTB. The W-2 wage and property basis limitations apply within the phase-out range. The IRS adjusts the annual TI threshold for inflation each year.

Sole proprietor and partnership TTS traders cannot pay themselves wages, so they likely cannot use the QBI phase-out range; however, they can make a QBI deduction below the threshold. For more information, see Chapter 17.

HEDGE FUNDS USE DUAL ENTITY STRUCTURE

U.S.-based hedge funds use partnerships (limited partnerships or LLCs filing partnership returns) for trading, usually S-Corps or C-Corps for their management company.

Partnerships are the best tax vehicle for a hedge fund because their tax filings allow "special allocations" for profit-allocation or carried-interest compensation to the manager instead of incentive advisory fees. Carried interest avoids suspended incentive fee deductions for investors. The S-Corp structure prohibits special allocations, and each owner must be treated equally with one ownership class. Retail business traders can trade in an S-Corp and receive employee-benefit deductions without needing a special allocation since there are no outside investors.

A hedge fund manager uses a management company to charge management fees and to arrange health insurance and retirement plan deductions for the owner/managers and other employees. Managers don't want all their business expenses reported on their hedge funds, as most costs belong to the management company. Retail trading businesses have more leeway; they deduct business expenses from the trading partnership or management company. Many investment managers prefer an S-Corp to reduce payroll taxes. (Read more about investment management taxes in Chapter 14.)

Partnership tax returns are more favorable vs. S-Corps on an owner basis and allocation of income and loss rules. By default, hedge funds use investor-level accounting with net asset value (NAV) and profit and loss allocated to each partner only when they are owners. That's not permissible with S-Corps. Again, while this is of utmost importance to a hedge fund, it's not an issue with trading your funds.

Bottom line: Hedge funds need a partnership structure and management company, and retail traders are better off with just an S-Corp trading company.

PROPRIETARY TRADING FIRMS USE PARTNERSHIP RETURNS

Proprietary trading firms are like hedge funds; they want "special allocations" on a partnership tax return. Generally, prop trader LLC owners don't share in firm-wide profits based on their percentage of ownership. Instead, the firm allocates profits based on their performance in a sub-trading account.

Proprietary trading firms differ significantly from retail entities and have unique legal, regulatory, business, and tax compliance needs. (Read more about proprietary trading in Chapter 12.)

ACCOUNTABLE PLAN FOR S-CORP

One formality of using an S-Corp is that it should have an accountable plan for reimbursing employee business expenses, including the employee's home office deduction. In 2018, TCJA suspended certain miscellaneous itemized deductions subject to the 2% floor, including unreimbursed employee business expenses, making an employer-provided accountable plan critical. At least the employer can deduct those expenses. With proper usage of an accountable plan, the S-Corp reports the deductions on its tax return. "Use or lose" the plan correctly before year-end.

Expense reporting is more relaxed with partnership tax structures. Partners may report unreimbursed partnership expenses on their individual tax return Schedule E, including home office deductions from Form 8829. S-Corp shareholders generally cannot deduct unreimbursed business expenses on Schedule E because the shareholders are categorized as employees when performing services for the corporation.

LIMITATIONS ON EXCESS BUSINESS LOSSES AND BUSINESS INTEREST EXPENSE

TCJA included an "excess business loss" (EBL) limitation of $500,000/$250,000 (married/other taxpayers) for 2018. The inflation-adjusted limit is $578,000/$289,000 (married/other taxpayers) for 2023 and $610,000/$305,000 (married/other taxpayers) for 2024. You can aggregate EBL from all pass-through businesses: A profitable company can offset another business with losses to remain under the limit. Other income and non-business losses do not affect the EBL calculation (i.e., capital gains and losses). EBL over the limit is an NOL carryforward.

The CARES Act suspended TCJA's EBL rules as they apply to the 2018, 2019, and 2021 tax years. The TCJA EBL rules return in 2023 through 2025 when TCJA changes expire. Recent tax laws extended these rules from 2025 to 2028.

Apply EBL at the partner or shareholder's level. The provision kicks in after implementing the passive loss rules, which don't apply to a trading company or hedge fund.

Here's an example of the EBL limitation for 2023: TTS/475 trader filing single has an ordinary loss of $500,000 for 2023. It's considered a business loss. This trader has income from wages of $100,000, so net EBL is $400,000. The 2023 EBL limitation is $289,000 for single, and the 2023 NOL carryover to 2024 is approximately $111,000 ($400,000 minus $289,000).

TCJA introduced a limitation on deducting business interest expense in Section 163(j). The 30% limitation should not impact most TTS traders because the $26 million three-year average "gross receipts" threshold applies to net trading gains. That's good news because if gross receipts used total sales proceeds on trades, a TTS trader with trading losses might have a business interest expense limitation. Since net trading gains are the standard for "gross receipts" in a trading business, only more substantial hedge funds might be impacted by the business interest expense limitation.

C-CORPS ARE NOT A GOOD CHOICE FOR TRADERS

Don't focus solely on the federal 21% flat tax rate on the C-Corp level. There are plenty of other taxes, including capital gains taxes on qualified dividends, state corporate taxes in 44 states, and accumulated earnings tax assessed on excess retained earnings.

When a C-Corp pays qualified dividends to the owner, double taxation occurs with capital gains taxes on the individual level (capital gains rates are 0%, 15%, or 20%). If an owner avoids paying sufficient qualified dividends, the IRS can assess a 20% accumulated earnings tax (AET).

C-Corps might not be able to use trader tax status (TTS), and if the IRS views them as an investment company, then no business deductions are allowed. (See our blog post, How to Decide if a C-Corp is Right for Your Trading Business https://tinyurl.com/ccorpyesorno).

Dual-entity solutions using a trading partnership and C-Corp management company are expensive and challenging to work in practice.

ASSET PROTECTION

Asset protection won't work in your home state if you have not registered your out-of-state company. If another party sues you, it's generally in your home state.

In our view, legal protection when trading your own money in an entity is not paramount since you don't have any customers or investors. However, investment managers managing other peoples' money most certainly need legal liability protection.

If you want asset protection, consider forming a trust in your home state. Convey interests in the entity to your trust. Proper insurance is essential, too. Consult with an attorney and insurance broker about liability protection under laws in your state.

Chapter 8

Retirement Plans

Traders use retirement plans in several ways.

They trade or invest within traditional retirement plans for tax-deferred growth. The ordinary income tax rate applies to withdrawals, and there's a 10% excise tax on "early withdrawals" made before age 59 ½. Required minimum distributions (RMD) must start by age 72. (73 if you reach age 72 after Dec. 31, 2022).

Traders like Roth IRAs and Roth 401(k)s because they are permanently tax-free and have no RMDs.

You can convert a traditional IRA or 401(k) into a Roth IRA but pay taxes on the value of the account converted.

TAX-ADVANTAGED GROWTH IN TRADITIONAL PLANS

Many Americans invest in financial markets via their 401(k), IRA, or other retirement plans. Take capital gains and losses within the traditional retirement plans with zero tax effect on current-year tax returns. Only withdrawals (or distributions) generate taxable income at ordinary tax rates. The retirement plan does not benefit from lower long-term capital gains rates. Traditional retirement plans aren't disenfranchised from deducting capital losses since reducing retirement plan amounts due to losses will eventually reduce taxable distributions accordingly.

EARNED INCOME IS NEEDED

Taxpayers can only make retirement-plan contributions if they have earned income, which is self-employment income or wage income. Trading gains are unearned income exempt from self-employment (SE) tax with individuals, partnerships, and S-Corps.

Futures traders who are full-fledged dealers/members of options or futures exchanges are an exception as they have "earned" income from their trading activity; their futures gains on that exchange are subject to SE tax (Section 1402i).

TTS traders can use an S-Corp trading company, eligible for trader tax status (TTS), to pay officer compensation and make retirement plan contributions. (See Chapter 7.)

SOLO 401(K) PLAN

Generally, the best retirement plan for a trader is a Solo 401(k) for TTS S-Corps established on the entity level in connection with officer compensation (payroll). It combines an "elective deferral"

(ED) contribution of $22,500 for 2023 and $23,000 for 2024. Plus, a profit-sharing plan contribution (PSP) up to a maximum of $43,500 for 2023 and $46,000 for 2024. The ED is 100% deductible and provides the main tax benefits. The PSP is 25% deductible, so $43,500 PSP divided by 25%-deductible equals a 2023 officer salary of $174,000. There is also a "catch-up provision" for taxpayers aged 50 and over of $7,500 for 2023 and 2024. The maximum contribution for those under age 50 is $66,000 for 2023 and $69,000 for 2024. For those 50 or older, it's $73,500 for 2023 and $76,500 for 2024.

You can contribute the ED component to a Roth Solo 401(k), forgoing taxable income deferral on a traditional contribution. The profit-sharing plan contribution is tax deductible as an expense of the S-Corp and must be traditional (not a Roth).

Traders need an entity to generate compensation; consider an S-Corp trading company. Employee benefits, including retirement and health insurance premiums, occur on the S-Corp level. TTS sole proprietors and partnerships cannot pay wages to the owners, so they cannot contribute to a retirement plan since they cannot create earned income from trading profits like with the S-Corp.

Many leading brokers offer Solo 401(k) plans on a cookie-cutter basis (which means "free"), and some allow active direct-access trading. Some traders cannot achieve in their Solo 401(k) plan the style of trading they do inside retail accounts, so they put off retirement plan contributions until later.

Traders often save thousands by deducting Solo 401(k) retirement plan contributions and health insurance premiums. (It's a higher saving when spouses work in the trading business and maximize retirement deductions.) Tax savings depend on income taxes saved versus payroll tax costs incurred.

PAYROLL TAX COSTS

Compensation is subject to payroll taxes (FICA and Medicare), which offset some of the income tax savings from the retirement plan contribution deduction. FICA is 12.4% of the Social Security base amount, limited to $160,200 for 2023 and $168,600 for 2024, and the Medicare portion (2.9%) is unlimited; it applies over the base amount. The employer and employee pay half of the FICA and Medicare taxes, and the employer has other minor payroll taxes. Consider a retirement plan contribution and deduction if the related income tax savings exceed payroll costs. S-Corp payroll taxes (the employer portion) are 100% deductible on the S-Corp tax return.

SOLO 401(K) IS BETTER THAN SEP IRA

A SEP IRA only has a profit-sharing plan with a maximum contribution of $66,000 for 2023 and $69,000 for 2024, and it doesn't have the $7,500 catch-up provision of the Solo 401(k).

To be allowed to contribute the maximum Solo 401(k) contribution of $66,000 (under age 50) for 2023, one needs officer compensation of $174,000 ($66,000 less $22,500 ED equals $43,500 divided by 25%). Conversely, to reach the maximum SEP IRA contribution, officer compensation of $264,000 is needed ($66,000 divided by 25%).

The lower compensation needed to maximize the Solo 401(k) means traders can save $2,610 of Medicare taxes on earned income (2.9% Medicare times the difference in compensation of $90,000). Net savings depend on the interplay between Medicare assessed on earned income vs. ACA's 3.8% Medicare surtax on net investment income — a trade-off.

The main reason for this payroll tax savings is that a trader can determine what amount of their trading gains are compensation, starting with none. Conversely, other types of small business income reported on a Schedule C or through a partnership tax return is earned income for SE tax, the equivalent of payroll tax, and it's often over the maximum needed anyway. Operating businesses like professional services using an S-Corp structure must adhere to "reasonable compensation" guidelines from the IRS. Still, traders can explain a lower compensation to the IRS because the underlying income is not SEI or earned income.

The most significant tax savings of the Solo 401(k) over a SEP IRA come from the elective deferral portion — income tax savings from a 100% deduction is far better than a 25% deduction. Many traders may not have high trading gains but earn enough to make the elective deferral part that saves the most money. Solo 401(k)s are only available to small businesses, establishing the plan before year-end. Pay the elective deferral portion by Jan. 31 (one month after deducting it through the December payroll) and pay the profit-sharing plan up until the due date of the tax return, including extension. One benefit of a SEP IRA is that you can establish it up until the due date of your tax return, including the extension. But it requires wages in an S-Corp, and you must execute payroll at year-end, so the extra time may not help.

Solo 401(k) plans require an annual 5500 or 5500-EZ filing if plan assets exceed $250,000, whereas IRAs and SEP IRAs do not have this filing requirement. If there are no outside employees in the Solo 401(k), taxpayers may use Form 5500-EZ. Don't miss that separate tax filing deadline of July 31 for calendar-year taxpayers. Taxpayers can file Form 5558 for an automatic two-and-a-half-month extension.

All IRAs, including SEPs and IRA rollovers, might trigger a wash-sale loss adjustment with individual taxable accounts, whereas a Solo 401(k) does not. (See this problem on wash sales in Chapter 4.)

DEFINED BENEFIT PLANS

Consistently high-income business owners, including trading businesses with owners/employees close to age 50, should consider a defined-benefit retirement plan (DBP) for significantly higher plan contributions and tax savings vs. a defined-contribution retirement savings plan (DCP) like a Solo 401(k).

DBP calculations are more complex than a DCP profit-sharing plan. An actuary must consider various factors in calculating retirement benefits and annual contributions. For more information, read Defined-Benefit Plans Offer Huge Tax Breaks (https://tinyurl.com/defined-benefit).

ANTI-DISCRIMINATION RULES

There's one caveat with all retirement plans: You need to cover all employees in your company and other "affiliated service groups" or "controlled groups," such as a related entity you own. Some traders hold the majority of equity in another business that hires many employees. They can't set up a high-deductible retirement plan for themselves in a trading entity without offering a similar benefit to their employees in that other business. Traders can limit this problem by using employee-vesting schedules. See https://tinyurl.com/retirement-how-to.

DOUBLE-UP STRATEGY

Those with a job in addition to trading can double their retirement savings by maximizing their employer 401(k) and contributing another $66,000 to an unaffiliated TTS S-Corp Solo 401(k) profit-sharing plan. See how in our article, How Some Traders Double-Up on Retirement Plan Contributions (https://tinyurl.com/double-up-plan).

DETERMINING APPROPRIATE OR REASONABLE COMPENSATION

S-Corp service companies should have "reasonable compensation" paid to the owner/employee. S-Corps don't pass through SE income or loss; they would avoid payroll taxes without reasonable compensation. Accounting industry practice for reasonable compensation is 25% to 50% of net income.

A trading company doesn't have underlying SE income, so reasonable compensation rules should not be a problem, although this can come up in an IRS notice or exam.

LOANS FROM QUALIFIED PLANS

While taxpayers can't borrow money from an IRA or SEP IRA because they are nonqualified plans, they can borrow money from a qualified plan like a Solo 401(k) or defined benefit plan for any reason. Many traders borrow money to add capital to their trading accounts.

Limitations and special rules: You can borrow up to a maximum of $50,000, limited to 50% of retirement plan assets. For example, if your Solo 401(k) has $80,000, you can borrow up to $40,000. If it has $120,000, you can borrow up to $50,000.

You must repay the loan on a quarterly fixed-amortization schedule over five years or less. You need a market rate of interest, and that interest is not tax deductible. Or, you may use the IRS applicable federal rates (AFR), which the IRS increased recently. Treat a loan not paid back as an ordinary income withdrawal. An early withdrawal from a qualified plan will incur a 10% excise tax penalty on Form 5329, included with a Form 1040 filing. Distributions are probably taxable in your home state, too. (Note: Early withdrawals from an IRA are up until age 59½.)

Suppose you leave your employer at age 55 or older. You may not be subject to the 10% early withdrawal penalty on a qualified plan like a 401(k), providing you follow "substantial periodic payment" rules. Otherwise, these distributions might blow up the retirement plan, making it all taxable income.

ROTH RETIREMENT ACCOUNTS AND CONVERSIONS

A Roth retirement plan is different from a traditional plan. The Roth has permanent tax savings on growth and contributions, whereas the conventional retirement plan only has deferral with taxes owed on total distributions during retirement. Distributions from a Roth plan are tax-free unless you take an early withdrawal that exceeds your non-deductible contributions over the years (be sure to keep accurate records).

Consider annual contributions to a Roth IRA. The rules are similar to traditional IRA contributions. Also, consider a Roth IRA conversion before year-end to maximize the use of lower tax brackets, offset business losses, and utilize itemized or standard deductions.

Here's an example: Assume a trader left their job at the end of 2023 and incurred trading losses in 2024 with trader tax status and Section 475 MTM ordinary loss treatment as a sole proprietor. Rather than carry forward an NOL under TCJA to subsequent years when there is an uncertain amount of income, this trader enacts a Roth IRA conversion before year-end 2024. They wind up paying some taxes within the low ordinary tax-rate brackets. If they skipped a Roth conversion, they would lose tax benefits on their standard or itemized deductions. This trader's Roth account will grow tax-free in 2024 and subsequent years.

If a converted Roth IRA account drops significantly in value after conversion, a taxpayer cannot reverse the Roth conversion. TCJA repealed the recharacterization option starting in 2018: "Recharacterization cannot be used to unwind a Roth conversion. However, recharacterization is still permitted with respect to other contributions. For example, an individual may contribute for a year to a Roth IRA and, before the due date for that year's individual's income tax return, recharacterize it as a contribution to a traditional IRA."

If there are market corrections in indexes and many individual stocks, consider a Roth conversion at those lower amounts to benefit from a potential recovery in markets inside the Roth

IRA, where that new growth is permanently tax-free. Converting at market bottoms is better than market tops. It's riskier without the reversal option anymore.

It's essential to pay conversion taxes from outside the Roth account; otherwise, the tax amount is an early withdrawal subject to the 10% excise tax. For example, if you convert $100,000, pay the conversion tax of $30,000 separately, and roll over the entire $100,000 to the Roth IRA, not $70,000 net of the taxes paid.

UNRELATED BUSINESS INCOME TAX

In some instances, activities within your retirement plans can bring about income taxes and unrelated business income taxes (UBIT), even though retirement plans are, by design, tax-free accounts. Be aware of potential tax traps.

When retirement plans contain activities not permitted by the Department of Labor (DOL) or Employee Retirement Income Security Act (ERISA), the IRS has various rules to tax a portion of these plans.

Your retirement accounts shouldn't pay you a fee for managing your funds; the IRS would deem that a prohibited transaction. I should point out that it's not self-dealing for your retirement plan to reimburse you for reasonable investment expenses. Such reimbursement might be a good idea because TCJA suspended investment fees and expenses as itemized deductions.

IRAs should be cash accounts (not margin accounts). Yet margin accounts are allowed for "qualified plans" such as a Solo 401(k).

Some brokers offer "margin type" IRA accounts permitting day trading on unsettled funds. However, these accounts don't provide overnight lending, and the broker does not charge margin interest expense. Some tax attorneys think these IRA accounts are not IRS-prohibited transactions, and there is no UBIT due to no margin interest paid. The same attorneys think these margin-type IRA accounts should pass muster with DOL, the IRA regulator.

Having a margin account alone doesn't trigger UBIT, but if personally guaranteed, it's considered a prohibited transaction. If one pays investment/margin-interest expense on securities within an IRA or qualified plan account, UBIT applies. Investment-interest expense only relates to trading securities on margin. Futures and forex may have notional leverage with higher risk, but that's not considered a margin-interest expense, so these accounts don't trigger UBIT issues (with one exception discussed in the next section).

Publicly traded ETFs, MLPs, and private hedge funds are pass-through entities requiring trust or partnership tax returns. They issue the investor a Schedule K-1, which passes through the character of the underlying tax matters to the investor. These ETFs, MLPs, and hedge funds may pay interest expense on their investments, which is passed on to a retirement plan investor. In that case, UBIT may be triggered. Avoidance of UBIT is why U.S. pension funds invest in offshore funds rather than domestic hedge funds; those offshore funds are known as UBIT blockers, as they are corporations without pass-through treatment.

Some MLPs conduct business activities, including energy, pipelines, and natural resources. When retirement plans invest in business activity, they must file separate tax forms (990-T) to report unrelated business income (UBI) and often owe UBIT. Many IRA owners are surprised to receive a Form 990-T requiring them to pay these taxes. Read my blog post, Retirement Plan Investments in Publicly Traded Partnerships Generate Tax Bills (https://tinyurl.com/retirement-ptp).

DO'S AND DON'TS

Traders can use intermediary retirement firm administrators offering non-prototype retirement plans to facilitate alternative investments like hedge funds, rental real estate, and certain types of self-directed trading. But be careful in choosing trust firms and carefully vet their content and suggested strategies. Many unscrupulous operators offer bad advice, like on IRA-owned LLCs with checkbook control and IRA-owned trust accounts with margin and personal guarantees. We believe such schemes are IRS-prohibited transactions and do not work. They can "blow up" a retirement plan, meaning the funds become taxable income and are subject to excise tax penalties.

Some traders may want to trade futures or forex in their retirement plans, but their brokers don't provide a method for that type of trading. Some brokers allow an arrangement with an intermediary retirement administration firm to open a trust trading account owned by your retirement plan. Such an arrangement should pass muster with futures — and on some forex accounts — since there's no margin interest paid to trigger UBIT or personal guarantees for a prohibited transaction. Some forex accounts have interest expense, whereas most have "rollover interest," which is not treated as interest expense (see Chapter 3).

Do not set up a trading business LLC owned by your IRA; that is a prohibited transaction. Read our related blog post (https://tinyurl.com/ira-do-dont) and watch our Webinar (https://tinyurl.com/ira-webinar).

Chapter 9

Tax Planning

Recent tax acts don't change trader tax status (TTS), Section 475 MTM accounting, wash-sale losses on securities, or the tax treatment on financial products, including futures (Section 1256 contracts) and cryptocurrencies (intangible property).

It's helpful to consider IRS inflation adjustments in income and capital gains tax brackets, various income thresholds and caps, retirement plan contribution limits, standard deductions, and more. See the article, IRS Provides Tax Inflation Adjustments for Tax-year 2024 (https://tinyurl.com/irs-inflation). The IRS increase for 2024 is about 7%.

EXCESS BUSINESS LOSSES AND NET OPERATING LOSSES

TTS traders with a Section 475 election might incur ordinary business losses for 2024. Before the Tax Cuts and Jobs Act (TCJA) started in 2018, a TTS/475 trader could carry back a net operating loss (NOL) for two years, generating a tax refund. TCJA introduced an "excess business loss" (EBL) limitation, with the excess being an NOL carryforward. TCJA repealed NOL carrybacks (except for farmers) and limited NOL carryforwards to 80% of the subsequent year's taxable income. CARES suspended TCJA's EBL and NOL changes for 2018, 2019, and 2020 and allowed five-year NOL carrybacks (i.e., a 2020 NOL carryback to 2015). TCJA's EBL and NOL carryforward rules apply for tax years 2021 through 2028.

DEFER INCOME AND ACCELERATE TAX DEDUCTIONS

Consider deferring income and accelerating tax deductions if you don't expect your taxable income to decline in 2025.

Traders eligible for TTS in 2024 should consider accelerating trading business expenses, such as purchasing equipment with first-year expensing using Section 179 or bonus depreciation.

Consider delaying sales of investments to defer capital gains. Defer bonuses at work.

ACCELERATE INCOME AND DEFER CERTAIN DEDUCTIONS

A TTS trader with substantial Section 475 ordinary losses should consider accelerating income to soak up the EBL. Try to advance enough income to use the standard deduction and take advantage of lower tax brackets. Stay below the threshold for unlocking various AGI-dependent deductions and credits. A higher income can lead to an Income-Related Monthly Adjustment Amount (IRMAA) adjustment, raising Medicare premiums.

ROTH IRA CONVERSION

Consider changing a traditional IRA or 401(k) into a Roth IRA. Distributions from a standard retirement plan are taxed as ordinary income (not capital gains), whereas with a Roth IRA, distributions are tax-free.

On the conversion date, the market value of the traditional retirement account is income taxed at ordinary rates. Futures growth and capital in the Roth IRA account are tax-free. If your retirement portfolio is depressed, you might enjoy recovery of values inside a Roth IRA.

Generally, there's a 10% excise tax on early withdrawals from retirement plans before age 59½. With a Roth IRA conversion, you can avoid excise tax by paying conversion taxes outside the Roth plan. TCJA repealed the recharacterization option, so you can no longer reverse the conversion if the plan assets decline. Roth IRA conversions have no income limit, unlike regular Roth IRA contributions.

As an illustration, a taxpayer filing single in 2024 has a $405,000 TTS/475 ordinary business loss. However, the excess business loss limitation for a single filing status in 2024 is $305,000 ($610,000 for married), so $100,000 is an NOL carryover to 2025. The taxpayer should consider a Roth conversion for 2024 to soak up most of the $305,000 allowed business loss and leave enough income to use the standard deduction and lower tax brackets.

ZERO TAX RATE ON LONG-TERM CAPITAL GAINS IN THE LOWEST TAX BRACKET

If you have a low income, consider realizing long-term capital gains by selling open positions held for more than 12 months. The 2024 long-term capital gains rates are 0% for taxable income in the 10% and 12% ordinary tax brackets. The 15% capital gains rate applies to the regular middle brackets, and the top capital gains rate of 20% applies to the top 37% ordinary income bracket. See capital gains tax brackets at https://taxfoundation.org/data/all/federal/2024-tax-brackets/ (look for IRS publishing the 2025 tax brackets in 2025). Remember, if you go $1 over the zero-rate bracket, all the long-term gains are subject to the 15% capital gains rate; it doesn't work like progressive marginal ordinary tax brackets.

NET INVESTMENT INCOME TAX

Investment fees and expenses are not deductible for calculating net investment income (NII) for the Affordable Care Act (ACA) 3.8% net investment tax (NIT). NIT only applies to individuals with NII and modified adjusted gross income (AGI) exceeding $200,000 single, $250,000 married filing jointly, or $125,000 married filing separately. The IRS does not index these ACA thresholds for inflation. NII includes portfolio income, capital gains, and Section 475 ordinary income.

BUSINESS EXPENSES AND ITEMIZED DEDUCTION VS. STANDARD DEDUCTION

Business expenses: TTS traders are entitled to business and home office deductions. The home office deduction requires income, except for the mortgage interest and real property tax portion. The SALT cap on state and local taxes does not apply to the home office deduction.

TCJA expanded first-year business property expensing; traders can deduct 100% of these costs in the year of acquisition, providing they place the item into service before year-end. Traders with TTS in 2024 may consider going on a shopping spree before Jan. 1. There is no sense in deferring TTS expenses because you cannot be sure you will qualify for TTS in 2025.

Employee business expenses: Ask your employer if they have an accountable plan for reimbursing employee-business costs. You must "use it or lose it" before year-end. TCJA suspended unreimbursed employee business expenses. TTS S-Corps should use an accountable plan to reimburse employee business expenses since the trader/owner is its employee.

Unreimbursed partnership expenses: Partners in LLCs taxed as partnerships can deduct unreimbursed partnership expenses (UPE). That is how they usually deduct home office expenses. UPE is more convenient than an S-Corp accountable plan because the partner can arrange the UPE after year-end. The IRS doesn't want S-Corps to use UPE.

SALT cap: TCJA capped state and local income, sales, and property taxes (SALT) at $10,000 per year ($5,000 for married filing separately) and did not index it for inflation. About 30 states enacted SALT cap workaround laws. Search "(Your state) SALT cap workaround" to learn the details for your state. Most states follow a blueprint approved by the IRS.

Generally, elect to make a "pass-through entity" (PTE) payment on a partnership or S-Corp tax return filed by your business. It doesn't work with a sole proprietorship filing a Schedule C. PTE is a business expense deduction shown on the state K-1 like a withholding credit. Most states credit the individual's state income tax liability with the PTE amount. Essentially, you convert a non-deductible SALT itemized deduction (over the cap) into a business expense deduction from gross income. Act well before year-end; otherwise, you might delay the benefit to next year.

Investment fees and expenses: TCJA suspended all miscellaneous itemized deductions subject to the 2% floor, which includes investment fees and expenses. TCJA left an itemized deduction for investment-interest expenses limited to investment income, with the excess as a carryover.

Standard deduction: TCJA roughly doubled the 2018 standard deduction and suspended and curtailed several itemized deductions. For 2024, with an inflation adjustment, the IRS increased the standard deduction to $29,200 for married filing jointly, $14,600 for single/married filing separately, and $21,900 for heads of household.

Many taxpayers use the standard deduction, simplifying their tax compliance work. For convenience, some taxpayers may feel inclined to stop tracking itemized deductions because they figure they will use the standard deduction. Don't overlook the impact of these deductions on state tax filings, where you might get some tax relief.

ESTIMATED INCOME TAXES

Those who have reached the SALT cap don't need to prepay 2024 state-estimated income taxes by Dec. 31, 2024 (a strategy before TCJA). Taxpayers should pay federal and state estimated taxes owed by Jan. 15, 2025, and the balance by April 15, 2025.

Many traders skip making quarterly estimated tax payments during the year, figuring they might incur trading losses later in the year. They can catch up with the Q4 estimate due by Jan. 15, 2025, but might still owe an underpayment penalty for Q1 through Q3 quarters. Some rely on the safe harbor exception to cover their prior year's taxes. (See Traders Should Focus On Q4 Estimated Taxes Due Jan. 18, https://tinyurl.com/yeys4fh6.)

ADJUST WITHHOLDING ON YEAR-END PAYCHECKS

Employees should consider withholding additional taxes on year-end paychecks, which helps avoid underpayment penalties since the IRS treats wage withholding as being made throughout the year. This loophole applies to officers/owners of TTS S-Corps.

AVOID YEAR-END WASH SALE LOSS ADJUSTMENTS

Taxpayers should report wash sale (WS) loss adjustments on securities based on "substantially identical" positions across all accounts, including IRAs. Substantially identical means equity, an option on that equity (equity option), and those options at different exercise dates.

Conversely, brokers assess WS only on identical positions per the one account and report on the 1099-B for that account. Active securities traders should use a trade accounting program to identify potential WS loss problems across all their accounts, especially going into year-end.

In taxable accounts, a trader can "break the chain" by selling the position before year-end and not repurchasing a substantially identical position 30 days before or after in any taxable or IRA accounts. Avoid WS between taxable and IRA accounts throughout the year, as that is a permanent WS loss.

Starting a new entity effective Jan. 1, 2025, can break the chain on individual account WS at year-end 2024, provided you don't purposely avoid WS with the related party entity. The new entity can also elect Section 475 MTM.

WS losses might be preferable to capital loss carryovers at year-end 2024 for TTS traders. A Section 475 election in 2025 converts year-end 2024 WS losses on TTS positions (not investment positions) into ordinary losses in 2025. That's better than a capital loss carryover into 2025, which might give you pause when making a 2025 Section 475 election. You want a clean slate with no remaining capital losses before electing Section 475 ordinary income and loss. (Learn how to read a broker 1099-B and wash sale loss adjustments in Chapter 4.)

TRADER TAX STATUS AND SECTION 475

Traders who qualified for TTS in 2024 may accelerate trading expenses into that qualification period as sole proprietors or entities. Those who don't qualify until 2025 should try to defer trading expenses until then. Traders may also capitalize and amortize (expense) Section 195 startup costs and Section 248 organization costs in the new TTS business, going back six months before commencement. TTS is a prerequisite for electing and using Section 475 MTM.

TTS traders choose Section 475 on securities to be exempt from wash-sale loss rules and the $3,000 capital loss limitation and be eligible for the 20% QBI deduction. To make a 2024 Section 475 election, individual taxpayers must have filed an election statement with the IRS by April 15, 2024 (March 15, 2024, for existing S-Corps and partnerships). If they filed that election statement on time, they must complete the election process by submitting a 2024 Form 3115 with their 2024 tax return to be filed in 2025. Those who missed the 2024 election deadline may want to consider the election for 2025. Capital loss carryovers are a concern — they can be used against capital gains but not Section 475 ordinary income. The 475 election remains in effect each year until revoked. The revocation process is similar to the election process.

A Section 475 election made by April 15, 2024, takes effect on Jan. 1, 2024. When converting from the realization (cash) method to the mark-to-market (MTM) method, you must prepare a Section 481(a) adjustment as of Jan. 1, 2024. The adjustment essentially reports in 2024 taxable income the unrealized capital gains and losses on open TTS securities positions held on Dec. 31, 2023. The adjustment does not apply to year-end investment positions, and those who don't qualify for TTS at year-end 2023 won't have a Section 481(a) adjustment to report for the 2024 tax year. A "new taxpayer" entity can elect Section 475 within 75 days of inception — a good option for those who miss the individual sole proprietor deadline (April 15, 2024). Forming a new entity on Nov. 1, 2024, or later is too late for establishing TTS for the 2024 year within the entity; we like to see all of Q4 for entity TTS eligibility at a minimum. Consider waiting until Jan. 1, 2025, to start a new TTS entity and elect Section 475 if it is late into 2024.

20% DEDUCTION ON QUALIFIED BUSINESS INCOME

In 2018, TCJA introduced a 20% qualified business income deduction (QBI). In a simple scenario, on a QBI of $100,000, the owner might be able to deduct $20,000. That's a tax deduction without spending any money.

Trading is a "specified service trade or business" (SSTB), which means an income cap applies. If your taxable income is over that cap, there is no QBI deduction. QBI includes Section 475 ordinary income, less TTS expenses, and excludes capital gains, portfolio income, and forex trading income.

Taxpayers can increase the QBI deduction with thoughtful year-end planning. Suppose taxable income falls within the phase-out range for a specified service activity or even above for a non-service business. You might need higher S-Corp wages (including officer compensation) to avoid a W-2 wage limitation on the QBI deduction. Deferring income can also help get under various QBI restrictions and thresholds. (Learn more about QBI in Chapters 2 and 7.)

SUSPENDING TTS AND SECTION 475

Assume a TTS/475 trader stopped trading on June 30, 2024. They must use Section 475 through June 30, 2024, but may not use it for the remainder of the year. TTS and 475 are "suspended" until and unless the trader is eligible again for TTS in a subsequent year. The trader can also revoke the 475 election for 2025 by April 15, 2025. Without 475 going into year-end 2024, the trader should try to avoid wash sale loss adjustments at year-end.

S-CORP OFFICER COMPENSATION

TTS traders use an S-Corp to arrange health insurance and retirement plan deductions. These deductions require earned income or self-employment income. A TTS S-corp salary is earned income, unlike unearned income trading gains.

S-Corps pay officer compensation in conjunction with employee benefit deductions through payroll tax compliance done before year-end 2024. Otherwise, traders miss the boat. TTS is necessary since an S-Corp investment company cannot have tax-deductible wages, health insurance, or retirement plan contributions. A trading S-Corp is not required to have "reasonable compensation," so a TTS trader may determine officer compensation based on how much to reimburse for health insurance and how much they want to contribute to a retirement plan. Remember, sole proprietor and partnership TTS traders cannot pay salaries to 2% or more owners; hence, they need an S-Corp.

S-Corp wages impact the SALT cap workaround, which hinges on net income after wages. If you fall into the QBI phase-out range, wages are required to increase the QBI deduction. This decision-making has many moving levers and parts, so consult your CPA for year-end tax planning in early December.

S-CORP HEALTH INSURANCE

S-Corps may only deduct health insurance for certain months, only the months it was operational and qualified for TTS. Employer-provided health insurance, including Cobra, is not deductible.

The S-Corp reimburses the employee/owner through the accountable reimbursement plan before year-end. Add the health insurance reimbursement to taxable wages, but do not withhold social security or Medicare taxes from that portion of W-2 compensation. The officer/owner takes an AGI deduction for health insurance on their tax return.

A taxpayer can deduct a contribution to a health savings account (HSA) without TTS or earned income.

S-CORP RETIREMENT PLAN CONTRIBUTION

TTS S-Corps can unlock a retirement plan deduction by paying sufficient officer compensation in December 2024 when results for the year are evident. Net income after deducting wages and retirement contributions should be positive.

If desired, you must establish a Solo 401(k) retirement plan for a TTS S-Corp with a financial intermediary before the year-end. Plan to pay the 100%-deductible "elective deferral" amount up to a 2024 maximum of $23,000 (or $30,500 if age 50 or older with the $7,500 catch-up provision) with the December 2024 payroll. That elective deferral is due by the end of January 2025. You can fund the 25% profit-sharing plan (PSP) portion of the S-Corp Solo 401(k) up to a maximum of $46,000 (subject to IRS increase) by the 2024 S-Corp tax return due date, including an extension, which means Sept. 15, 2025. The maximum PSP contribution requires wages of $184,000 ($46,000 divided by a 25% defined contribution rate). Tax planning calculations will show the various options' projected outcome of income tax savings vs. payroll tax costs.

Consider a Solo 401(k) Roth for the elective-deferral portion only, where the contribution is not deductible, but the contribution and growth within the Roth are permanently tax-free. Traditional plans have a tax deduction upfront, and all distributions are subject to ordinary income taxes in retirement.

Traditional retirement plans have required minimum distributions (RMD) by age 72 (73 if you reach age 72 after Dec. 31, 2022), whereas Roth plans don't have RMD.

HAVE YOUR NEW ENTITY READY ON JAN. 1, 2025

If you missed employee benefits (health insurance and retirement contributions) in 2024, consider an LLC with an S-Corp election for the tax year 2025. Or maybe you want a spousal-member LLC taxed as a partnership for 2025 to maximize the SALT cap workaround and segregate trading from investing.

If you want the new entity to be ready to trade on the first trading day of January 2025, consider the following plan. Form a single-member LLC in December 2024, obtain the employee identification number (EIN) online, and open the LLC brokerage account before year-end to be ready to trade as of Jan. 1, 2025. The single-member LLC is a "disregarded entity" for the tax year 2024, which avoids an entity tax return filing for the 2024 initial short year. You can add your spouse as an LLC member on Jan. 1, 2025, creating a partnership tax return for 2025.

If you want health insurance and retirement plan deductions for 2025, then your single-member or spousal-member LLC should submit a 2025 S-Corp election within 75 days of Jan. 1, 2025.

The partnership or S-Corp is a "new taxpayer" to make an internal resolution to elect Section 475 MTM on securities only for 2025 within 75 days of Jan. 1, 2025. Otherwise, existing partnerships or S-Corps must file an external 475 election statement with the IRS by March 15, 2025.

TAX-LOSS HARVESTING

If you have an investment or trading portfolio, you can reduce capital gains taxes via "tax-loss harvesting" before the year-end. If you realized significant capital gains year-to-date in 2024 and have open positions with substantial unrealized capital losses, consider selling some of those losing positions to reduce 2024 taxes on capital gains.

Be sure to wait 30 days to repurchase those securities to avoid wash sale loss adjustments, which would postpone the 2024 year-end tax loss to 2025, thereby defeating the concept of tax loss selling.

You don't have to wait if you buy a similar security, providing it's not "substantially identical." For example, an exchange-traded fund (ETF) like SPY is substantially identical to options on SPY (the derivative) but not to other ETFs that track the S&P 500. The symbol SPX is a stock index future, a Section 1256 contract, which is not a security, so that's okay to use to avoid wash sales.

TAX EFFICIENT SALES

If you want to sell some of your portfolios, consider taking long-term capital gains subject to lower tax rates (0%, 15%, and 20%) vs. short-term capital gains taxed at ordinary rates. That might require using the "specific identification accounting method" vs. first-in-first-out. (See Chapter 4.)

STRADDLES AND CONSTRUCTIVE SALE RULES

The IRS has rules to prevent the deferral of income and acceleration of losses in offsetting positions that lack sufficient economic risk. These rules include straddles, the constructive sale rule, and shorting against the box. Also, be aware of the "constructive receipt of income" — you cannot receive payment for services, turn your back on that income, and defer it to the next tax year.

Selling the losing legs on a complex options trade with offsetting positions can trigger the straddle loss deferral rules.

CHARITABLE CONTRIBUTIONS

Consider a charitable remainder trust to bunch philanthropic contributions for itemizing deductions. (Ask Fidelity or Schwab about it.)

You may also donate appreciated securities to charity. You get a charitable deduction at the fair market value and avoid capital gains taxes. (This is a strategy billionaires use, and you can use it, too.)

Consider directing your traditional retirement plan to make "qualified charitable distributions." That satisfies the RMD rule, and it's not taxable income. It's the equivalent of an offsetting charitable deduction, allowing you to take the standard deduction rather than itemize charitable contributions.

In 2020 and 2021, the limit on charitable contributions increased to 100% of AGI. The limit reverts to the 60% limit for 2024 and subsequent years. (See the IRS site for Charitable Contribution Deductions.)

TAX RELIEF: PRESIDENTIALLY DECLARED DISASTER AREAS

There might be disasters in 2024, including hurricanes and wildfires. Check the irs.gov site for Tax Relief in Disaster Situations. Taxing authorities update the tax filing and payment deadlines in disaster areas, so watch their websites.

Chapter 10

Dealing with the IRS and States

The IRS and states have processes for inquiries (notices), exams (audits), appeals, and tax courts.

TAX NOTICES AND EXAMS

When a tax notice arrives, don't panic and rush to reply to an IRS agent. Understand where the IRS is coming from; it may be a computer-generated notice asking for a few simple open items. If the IRS is getting ready to challenge TTS and Section 475 MTM, it's essential to step back and make sure you have a strong case for TTS qualification and that you elected Section 475 correctly by the deadline.

Don't expect the IRS to get it right the first time around. The notice may have a hobby-loss business or passive-loss activity questionnaire, and a trading business is exempt from those rules. Agents often calculate volume, frequency, and other metrics on your trading activity to determine TTS qualification in ways that are favorable to them and wrong in our view, so do the calculations right.

If you made an error on your tax return but qualified for TTS and elected Section 475 MTM on time, you may be able to fix things quickly. On the other hand, if you're a close call on TTS and potentially messed up your Section 475 MTM election or other matters, consider getting representation from a trader tax expert.

EXAM RECONSIDERATION IS UNLIKELY

Traders can reply with a "reconsideration" request, asking the IRS to close its exam before it gets underway. If the trader filed a Schedule C with a loss, even though they had trading gains over expenses, it might be easy to get the exam closed (assuming he qualifies for TTS). Other types of notices or exams can be completed with little work, too.

The solution can be as simple as filing a corrected tax return with the proper tax treatment, i.e., filing Form 4797 rather than MTM losses incorrectly on Schedule C and including a detailed footnote. (Providing you elected Section 475 MTM on time.)

We haven't noticed many IRS exams being reconsidered lately. It seems the IRS agent wants to delve into the items listed on the tax notice. It's essential to keep the agent on the subject and limit their scope so it doesn't grow to more areas of your tax return or more years. Once the IRS finds a problem, it often seeks to expand the exam to prior and subsequent tax years.

IRS notices may include questions about business status. However, these agents often use standard questions to assess "hobby-loss" treatment. TTS requires the intention to run a business, thereby trumping the hobby-loss rules. Trading is not a recreational or personal activity, two critical requirements for a hobby-loss business.

APPEALS

Expect the IRS agent to deny TTS unless you have a clear-cut case. Agree to disagree with the agent and go to the appeals level. Show the appeals officer how you are prepared to go to tax court to win based on the application of trader tax court cases. It's best to have a trader tax expert CPA or attorney in your corner to present your TTS qualification, explain trader tax law, and prepare the appeals letter. Like most tax preparers, most IRS agents and appeals officers are not well versed in trader tax law, and many might misapply tax court cases. Be prepared to negotiate in appeals but hang tough to win a favorable outcome. The appeals letter should be professional and serve as a precursor to the petition to file for tax court. That will earn respect from the appeals officer, and they will take you more seriously.

TRANSFER THE EXAM OR APPEALS

If you work with a CPA firm well-versed in trader tax exams, consider transferring the exam or appeal to that CPA. They probably have excellent experience working with local IRS appeals and educated the IRS agents on TTS and Section 475 elections.

TAX COURT

If appeals deny TTS and Section 475 MTM, and your trader tax expert thinks you have a good case with a lot of money on the line, then consider filing a petition in tax court. We usually suggest a "small case" filing. Engage the trader tax expert to write the tax court petition — preferably a tax attorney well versed in trader tax law.

A client engaged our CPA firm after making errors in his self-prepared tax return filing, inviting an IRS audit, and mishandling the agent and appeals officer. After a consultation, we felt he qualified for TTS and elected Section 475 MTM on time. Our tax attorney had less than a week to write the petition for tax court. The IRS considered our petition, conceded, and closed the case, abating (removing) a tax bill for well over $100,000. Most trader tax court cases were cases where we feel the trader did not qualify for TTS. The best strategy is to claim TTS only when you qualify for it and elect Section 475 MTM correctly. (Read trader tax court cases in Chapter 11.)

STATES ALSO SEND TAX NOTICES AND INITIATE EXAMS

We've noticed more states challenging TTS and related tax breaks independently, without the IRS taking the lead. Arizona tried to apply hobby-loss rules to a bonafide trading business; we said that was wrong, and the state eventually agreed with us. Most states are based on or coupled with federal tax law, and they should not depart from federal tax law when they feel it's convenient. California and a few other state tax authorities initiated a state tax exam to challenge TTS for a few of our clients. In these situations, we had two choices: try to get the exam reconsidered (closed), claim TTS is an IRS matter (which probably won't work), or present a case to win as we would with the IRS. We chose the latter and prevailed. When the IRS or state changes your taxes, they advise the other tax authority, so expect federal and state damage on a negative tax adjustment.

A few states and local tax authorities have entity-level taxes based on gross receipts or gross margin. In many cases, trading gains are exempt as portfolio income on the sale of capital assets (non-business) rather than business-earned income. In other instances, gross margin may include trading gains.

See our blog for more on defending trader tax: https://tinyurl.com/defend-trader-tax.

IRS INITIATIVES

The IRS has a few initiatives focused on traders.

1099-B matching to Form 8949: The IRS might develop the capability to match cost-basis reporting on 1099-Bs with taxpayer Form 8949s. There are many complexities in cost-basis reporting on securities, including wash sales. Traders might receive tax notices with questions about the differences between 1099-Bs and Form 8949.

Suppose a taxpayer complies with Section 1091 rules requiring wash-sale calculations based on substantially identical positions (between stocks and options) across all accounts, including IRAs. In that case, the taxpayer will likely have discrepancies with broker 1099-Bs based on identical positions (same symbol) for wash sales losses calculated on an individual account basis only. In this case, you should include a tax return footnote explaining the difference between the IRS wash-sale loss rules for brokers vs. taxpayers. You don't have to account for each difference per line item.

(Read about the issues with cost-basis reporting, Form 8949, Form 1099-Bs, and wash sales in Chapter 4.)

Attacks on trader tax status: The IRS might challenge sole proprietor TTS traders because they only report business expenses on Schedule C, not trading income reported on other tax forms. Their Schedule C looks like a losing business. Sole proprietor business traders with significant ordinary losses from trading expenses and Section 475 MTM losses may hear from the IRS since such losses will likely generate substantial net operating losses (NOLs). NOL carryback refund claims garner more attention than carryforwards. TCJA repealed NOL carrybacks starting in 2018; however, CARES temporarily overrode TCJA, allowing five-year NOL carrybacks in 2018, 2019, and 2020. Other attention grabbers are perennial money-losing traders and errors on tax return filings on TTS, Section 475, tax treatment, and missing footnotes.

The IRS has been underfunded, and the number of agents is down; computer matching and computer-generated tax notices are taking up some slack. The 2023 Inflation Reduction Act (IRA) includes an IRS plan to hire 87,000 new employees.

We hope more traders assess TTS correctly. Don't play the audit lottery by trying to cheat the IRS and your state on tax treatment. Cheating gives the trading industry a bad name and complicates our job. If you have trouble with the IRS or your state, please consult an expert.

With TCJA suspending investment expenses, more taxpayers might attempt to claim TTS. Others will form a dual-entity structure with an investment partnership and management company. Unless outside clients exist, the IRS may scrutinize these family office structures and deny business expense treatment.

Section 475 improper identification. The IRS and some states have been playing havoc with traders in exams, claiming they did not correctly comply with Section 475 rules for segregating investment positions from trading positions. Noncompliance allows the agent to drag misidentified investment positions into Section 475 mark-to-market (MTM) as trading positions. Or to reclassify misidentified trading losses from Section 475 into investment capital-loss treatment subject to the $3,000 capital-loss limitation. Both exam changes can cause substantial tax bills, penalties, and interest expenses.

Traders don't want to lose capital gains deferral and lower long-term capital gains rates on investment positions in securities. With misidentified investments, the IRS can drag positions into Section 475, subjecting them to MTM and ordinary income tax rates.

Section 475 contains a clause to limit unrealized losses on investment positions dragged into Section 475. Suppose you misidentify a trade as an investment. Any unrealized loss would be recognized only against other Section 475 gains, and you would defer the excess until selling the security.

TTS traders with Section 475 MTM can prevent this problem by carefully identifying each investment position contemporaneously. When you receive confirmation of purchasing an investment position, email yourself to identify it as an investment position, as that constitutes a timestamp in your books and records. Don't hold onto winning Section 475 trading positions and morph them into investment positions, as that does not comply with the rules. If identifying each particular investment is inconvenient, then ring-fence investments into identified investment accounts vs. active trading accounts. Use "do not trade" lists for investing vs. trading accounts so you don't trade the same symbol in both accounts.

But this compliance is not enough. If you trade actively around your investments, the IRS can say you failed to segregate the investment in substance.

Entities navigate around the problem. The simple fix is to form a single-member or spousal-member LLC with an S-Corp election or a spousal LLC taxed as a partnership. Conduct all business trading with Section 475 on securities in those entity accounts. (The entity may elect Section 475 MTM internally within 75 days of inception.) Reported on the S-Corp tax return are trader tax status, business expenses, and Section 475 trading gains and losses.

Avoiding investment positions in the entity accounts is wise. However, some traders want to use portfolio margining, and brokers don't allow that between individual and entity accounts, so they want to transfer some prominent investment positions into the entity accounts. That can become a problem for Section 475 segregation of investment rules, especially if you trade the same symbols. Sometimes, a trader must choose between portfolio margining or Section 475.

Keep investments in your investment accounts. The individual and entity accounts are not connected for purposes of Section 475 rules since they are separate taxpayer identification numbers. (See more in Chapter 2 relating to Section 475).

DON'T LET THE IRS FILE YOUR RETURN

If you trade securities, the IRS receives a broker-issued 1099-B that shows proceeds on "covered securities" plus cost-basis information. Due to the cost-basis reporting requirements, the IRS has a clearer picture of trading gain or loss.

File your tax returns before the IRS contacts you, enhancing your chances of reduced penalties. While if you have reasonable cause, you should seek abatement of penalties, interest is statutory. File your late returns as soon as possible, reporting capital losses. Then, you can carry over capital losses to subsequent tax years, which isn't possible unless you file the prior year's tax returns. Don't wait more than three years; it will be too late to apply capital loss and NOL carryovers.

If you can't pay your taxes on time, at least file on time and request an installment plan (Form 9465); you can make corrections later. Failing to file an automatic tax extension is a mistake because "late filing" penalties are much higher than "late payment" penalties.

Be honest and forthright with the IRS; don't ignore it. Forget about cheating on your taxes with offshore or other schemes.

AVOID BAD ADVICE

Sadly, many traders don't handle their tax affairs correctly, and often, trusted "professionals" and tax software providers underserve them.

An accountant working in a nationally branded tax storefront or local CPA firm may not be qualified to deliver trader tax services. We have seen many cases where traders have gotten into tax trouble using tax providers who don't know trader tax. Some storefronts offer audit guarantees but don't pay back taxes or pay a new CPA to fix things. That's a hollow guarantee. How can you recover lost tax savings with these "professionals"? Others offer free reviews, but what good is that offer if the person doesn't know trader tax benefits and rules? "Free" often means an opportunity to sell something you may not need, like a dual entity scheme.

Far too many active traders miss out on trader tax benefits — they don't deduct allowable business expenses or elect and use ordinary-loss treatment on time. They overpay and don't receive their tax refunds. Even when they do most things right, they file a return with a red flag, causing an exam.

Conversely, some accountants professing to be trader tax experts disrespect TTS and set up schemes for investors to misuse business treatment and Section 475 MTM. Their clients don't qualify for TTS, and they face a heap of trouble from the IRS in an exam.

You need an experienced trader tax expert in your corner to handle this challenging IRS environment.

AVOID IRS PROBLEMS BY USING AN ENTITY

There are a few tips for dealing with the IRS. The most important ones are to get help before setting up your trading business and to get help preparing your tax returns. The process includes considering the best entity structure, dealing with startup costs properly, adopting tax reporting strategies to reduce red flags, and explaining your TTS and treatment in well-written footnotes accompanying the return. A proper business setup and trader tax return filed on time will generally not be questioned, except for those with massive ordinary losses, especially NOL carrybacks (2017 and prior years). Starting in 2018, TCJA required NOL carryforwards. However, CARES permitted five-year NOL carryback refund claims for 2018, 2019, and 2020 NOLs.

CRYPTOCURRENCIES

Congress and the IRS enacted several initiatives to stop noncompliance with cryptocurrencies. The IRS sent out tax notices to taxpayers involved with cryptocurrencies. They added questions about cryptocurrencies to Form 1040 income tax returns, including criminal and civil penalties if skipped. The SEC and CFTC promise new cryptocurrency regulations to rein in the Wild West. See https://tinyurl.com/virtual-currency.

Chapter 11

Traders in Tax Court

The IRS did an excellent job in recent trader tax court cases (Obayagbona, Poppe, Assaderaghi, Nelson, and Endicott), laying out the trader tax laws and requirements for qualification and in its analysis of the taxpayers. These cases also involved missed or botched Section 475 elections.

The Poppe court (October 2015) awarded trader tax status (TTS) with 720 trades (60 trades per month). Obayagbona had insufficient volume and frequency of transactions, and the court agreed with the IRS to deny TTS.

The Assaderaghi, Nelson, and Endicott courts denied TTS and the other tax breaks that hinged on it. The facts of those cases were similar: All three defendants managed their substantial investments with options and were not TTS traders. The IRS recap of trader tax law presented in these cases was informative. There are more precise lines for options traders not to cross, like the average holding period of 31 days (Endicott), over 720 total trades (Poppe), and frequency of trade executions on approximately 75% of available trading days. One critical lesson in these cases is to segregate investment activity from trading business activity. Otherwise, it all looks like an investment program.

Taxpayers should bring moderate and winning cases to tax court. The lesson of the Obayagbona, Poppe, Assaderaghi, Nelson, and Endicott cases is that taxpayers without professional representation or with tax attorneys who lack trader tax expertise should not bring losing cases to tax court. If you're dealing with IRS or state tax controversy and want to know how to proceed, read Chapter 10. Also, see our blogs: Another Non-business Trader Busted in Tax Court (https://tinyurl.com/nelson-gtt) and Tax Court Was Right to Deny Endicott TTS (https://tinyurl.com/gtt-endicott).

OBAYAGBONA VS. COMMISSIONER

Obayagbona was far off the mark with insufficient volume and frequency of trades and was denied TTS on Nov. 3, 2016.

Volume: Obayagbona had 253 total trades in 2008 and 252 total in 2009. That's less than half the 720 approved in the Poppe court.

Frequency: Our golden rules call for trades on 75% of available trading days, and Obayagbona was under 50%. The court emphasized frequency in this case.

POPPE VS. COMMISSIONER

Let's break down the William F. Poppe vs. Commissioner court case (Oct. 19, 2015, T.C. Memo. 2015-205). In addition to the number of trades per annum, Poppe seems to have satisfied our other golden rules on frequency, the average holding period, intention to run a business, serious account size, material equipment, business expenses, and more. Plus, Poppe had a good background as a stockbroker. Poppe was a teacher and part-time trader for several years, fitting trading into his schedule. It helped that he made a lot of money trading in a few years compared to his teacher's salary.

Botched Section 475 election. Poppe had substantial trading losses ($1 million in 2007) for which he claimed Section 475 ordinary business loss treatment rather than a puny $3,000 capital-loss limitation against other income. But like other tax court cases (Assaderaghi, Nelson, Endicott, Holsinger, and Chen), the tax court busted Poppe for either lying to the IRS about making a timely Section 475 election or making a valid election but not being able to prove it to the IRS. Poppe never filed a required Form 3115 to perfect the Section 475 election, which begs the question: Did he ever file an election statement on time?

The case opinion states that Poppe intended to elect Section 475 for 2003 and filed his 2003 tax return late in 2005, omitting a required 2003 Form 3115. Poppe's tax preparer reported 2003 Section 475 trading gains on Schedule C. That's incorrect and a red flag: Report Section 475 trading gains on Form 4797 Part II ordinary gain or loss. This botched reporting indicates that Poppe's tax preparer did not understand Section 475 tax law, which probably buttressed the IRS win.

Many traders are in the same predicament as Poppe and should do their best to document the election filing in case the IRS challenges it. We also provide the election process for our clients and ask them to record their filings. Send an email with the relevant facts, as the email has a timestamp. Safeguard a copy of the election and Form 3115 in your permanent files.

Poppe's errors in Section 475. Poppe could not verify the external 475 election statement (step one) or a Form 3115 filing (step two). It wasn't just a question of being late on a Form 3115 filing; Poppe never filed one, and he was an existing taxpayer individual.

Traders should file the external Section 475 election statement with a certified return receipt. But that may not be enough because it only verifies a mailing containing the tax return or extension. The IRS recognized this problem and suggested taxpayers include a perjury statement on Form 3115 stating they filed the 475 election on time.

Is there any relief from the IRS? My colleague Darren Neuschwander, CPA, spoke with an IRS official a few years ago who said the IRS had granted some relief to a few traders provided they were only a little late with their Form 3115 filing, but they filed the election statement on time. The IRS official pointed out there is no relief for filing the election statement late.

But Poppe was not a little late — he never filed a Form 3115. It's wise to file Form 3115 on time per the written rules and not rely on hearsay about possible relief from IRS officials, which may no longer be granted after the Poppe decision.

Proprietary trading account or disguised customer account? The court construed Poppe's proprietary trading firm arrangement as a disguised retail customer account. This ruling should be a concern for the proprietary trading firm industry, especially since regulators warned clearing firms about disguised customer accounts in the past. By agreement, prop traders do not trade their capital in a retail customer account. They trade a firm sub-account with firm capital and far higher inter-firm leverage than is available with a retail customer account. See more about this in Chapter 14 on proprietary trading firms.

ASSADERAGHI VS. COMMISSIONER

The IRS is piling up victories in tax court against individual traders who inappropriately use Section 475 MTM business ordinary loss treatment for deducting significant trading losses. Fariborz Assaderaghi & Miao-Fen Lin v. Commissioner (Feb. 25, 2014, T.C. Memo. 2014-33) is one of them. According to Tax Analysts, "The Tax Court held that a husband's trading activity in securities didn't constitute a trade or business and, thus, he wasn't eligible for a mark-to-market accounting method election under section 475(f), and the couple was limited to a $3,000 deduction of losses from the purchase and sale of securities under section 1211(b) for each year at issue."

Only traders who qualify for TTS (Schedule C business expenses) may elect and use Section 475. A lot is at stake since, without TTS or a timely Section 475 MTM election, traders use a puny $3,000 capital loss limitation against other income.

We agree with the IRS that Assaderaghi did not qualify for TTS in any of the years examined. Assaderaghi had many day trades and used professional trading equipment and charts. But he had a demanding full-time career as an engineer/executive, and the IRS is more skeptical toward part-time traders claiming TTS. Assaderaghi could not prove his hours spent in trading, and his evidence lacked credibility in the eyes of the IRS and tax court.

Most importantly, Assaderaghi came up short of meeting our golden rules for 2008, the one year he had a chance to qualify for TTS. He had 535 trades (we now recommend 720 total trades). He traded over 60% of available trading days (our golden rules call for trade executions on 75% of available trading days). In the other years examined, he came up far short of TTS, which displayed a feeble case when considering the years together.

Perhaps Assaderaghi could have fought harder to win TTS in 2008 and conceded the other years, but that was not the main issue. The more significant issue was filing a timely Section 475 MTM election, which Assaderaghi and his accountant did not do. Not fling the election was important because Assaderaghi's CPA deducted $374,000 in trading losses on his 2008 Schedule C, a red flag. Still, the IRS forced them to use a puny $3,000 capital loss limitation instead since no valid Section 475 election was made for 2008. Once again, a trader and professional went to a tax court with a losing case on technical grounds, and nothing could be done about it. They caved on TTS when perhaps they could have won that part of the exam.

Assaderaghi made some tragic rookie tax mistakes. He asked his local CPA tax preparer to elect TTS and Section 475 MTM, but after not getting an answer from his CPA, he didn't do anything about it. His accountant was clueless about trader tax benefits and rules — which is sadly still often the case. Regarding timely Section 475 elections, there is no excuse for relying on an accountant and no IRS relief. The IRS is lenient on many things, but not Section 475 elections.

His accountant grasped the idea of trading as a business, but he concluded that he could report trading gains and losses on Schedule C like other companies. He should have filed for Section 475 and reported trading gains and losses on Form 4797 Part II with ordinary income and loss treatment. The accountant did not know that an individual TTS trader had to elect Section 475 MTM for 2008 by April 15, 2008, and perfect it with a 2008 Form 3115 change of accounting filed in 2009 with the 2008 tax returns.

Assaderaghi's tax return screamed for an IRS beatdown. The IRS computers saw trading losses on Schedule C and issued a tax notice. The IRS tried to match broker 1099-Bs to Schedule D (in 2008 and Form 8949 after 2010), Form 4797 Part II (section 475 MTM), and Form 6781 (Section 1256), but none were correctly reported on these forms. The IRS agent asked the CPA preparer about a Section 475 MTM election, and the CPA did not even know what the agent was talking about. Case closed — it's a loser! You can never file a Section 475 MTM election late.

An exception is a six-month extension for filing a Section 475 election based on "Section 9100 relief." It requires filing a private letter ruling (PLR), but the IRS has rejected PLRs for this, except for Larry Vines, who had no prejudice or hindsight. See Chapter 2.

Lessons learned: Learn trader tax benefits and rules with our content and hire a proven trader tax CPA to assist you with qualification for TTS, a Section 475 election, Form 3115, Form 4797, and tax return footnotes.

This case does not change our golden rules. The Assaderaghi court reinforced that business traders must be consistent in trading volume and frequency and avoid sporadic lapses in active trading. The tax law requires "regular, frequent and continuous trading based on daily market movements and not long-term appreciation."

Consider forming an entity that qualifies for TTS and files an entity business tax return that resembles many active trading hedge funds. As pointed out in this guide, a high-ranking IRS person in the TTS and Section 475 area warned at a tax conference that the IRS is going after individual traders inappropriately using TTS and Section 475 MTM ordinary loss treatment. Get the help you need to be a winner.

CHEN VS. COMMISSIONER (2004)

It's been almost 20 years since this case went to tax court, but an IRS official reiterated the importance of it, deeming similar circumstances "Chen cases." The IRS official referred to sole proprietor traders reporting large Schedule C and Form 4797 (Section 475) ordinary losses on individual tax returns and filing for large NOL carryback refund claims with the IRS. All the cases in this chapter are similar: individuals with Schedule C and Form 4797 losses. It's much better to file as an entity trader with Section 475. There may be a silver lining to TCJA's repeal of NOL carrybacks and introduction of an excess business loss (EBL) limitation with NOL carryforward: The IRS might have fewer reasons to initiate a tax exam against TTS traders. (CARES temporarily allowed five-year NOL carrybacks and waived EBL rules for 2018, 2019, and 2020.)

Chen was a part-time trader with a full-time job who entered and exited his trading business in three months after losing almost all his money in hyperactive trading.

Chen botched many things in this case. First and foremost, he lied to the IRS about electing Section 475(f) MTM on time and then used MTM when he wasn't eligible. Second, Chen brought a losing case to tax court and made the mistake of representing himself. Once the IRS busted Chen on the phony MTM election, he caved in on all points, including TTS.

The problem for traders is that once MTM ordinary loss treatment is lost — by far the most significant tax benefit on the line — poorly represented traders in tax court too readily concede TTS, which may only deliver another $5,000 of tax benefits. If you're paying for legal counsel, why continue to pay an attorney to win just a few thousand dollars of tax benefits?

Even though Chen only traded for three months while keeping his full-time job, it doesn't mean he didn't start a new business — to change careers to business trading — and make a total investment of time, money, and activity. Tax code or case law doesn't state that a business must be carried on for a whole year or as the primary means of making a living. Countless companies start and fail in a few short months, and often, the entrepreneur hasn't left their job while experimenting as a businessperson. Chen may have won TTS had he been upfront with the IRS and engaged a tax attorney or trader tax expert to represent him in court. Chen never filed a 475 election.

Chen vs. Commissioner is relevant for recent years with the advent of pandemic-fueled traders commencing TTS in Q2 or Q3 2020. Will these new traders have enough longevity in the business to be eligible for TTS? (See our article, Will the IRS Deny Tax Benefits to Traders Due to Covid?, https://tinyurl.com/covid-traders.)

HOLSINGER VS. COMMISSIONER (2008)

Holsinger was a close call at best on TTS. (Our CPA firm would not have allowed TTS if we had been preparing his tax returns, as he fell short of our golden rules based on the facts we learned in his sub-par presentation to the court.)

Holsinger also made several errors on his tax return, which rightfully drew IRS attention and an exam. Holsinger formed a spousal-member LLC for his trading business and correctly filed an internal MTM election on the entity. The problem: Holsinger never traded in the LLC's name; instead, he traded in a joint individual account with his wife. He didn't elect 475 MTM on a personal level, so the IRS easily won the denial of 475 MTM in tax court.

Holsinger has similarities to Chen. Holsinger wasn't entitled to use MTM, yet he used it anyway and tried to defend it in tax court. Like Chen, Holsinger got off the wrong foot and lost credibility with the IRS. He unsuccessfully argued that he individually acted as an "agent" for the LLC. Also, he was retired, which raises the bar on TTS qualification in the eyes of the IRS, as is the case with part-time and money-losing traders.

Holsinger's total trades were less than 320 — well below our golden rule, which requires 720 total trades at a minimum. Holsinger's average holding period was more than one month, but it must be under 31 days per the Endicott court. His total cost basis on trades was well under $1 million per year, which is low by trader tax standards. TTS traders usually have cost basis and proceeds of more than several million dollars per year, indicating rapid turnover and materiality.

In the Holsinger decision, the IRS cited the usual tax court cases on TTS, which included a broad range of total trades. On one end of the spectrum, one court case denied TTS on fewer than 100 total trades. Conversely, the IRS agreed to TTS with 1,100 total trades. Holsinger fell somewhere in the lower middle. Holsinger traded on only 40% of available trading days in 2001 and 45% in 2002. Our golden rules call for 75% frequency.

CONTINUOUS BUSINESS ACTIVITY

Unfortunately, these past few years, we didn't make any headway with our "continuous business activity" (CBA) argument on easing qualification for TTS (business treatment). We've been hoping it can help many traders who face challenging qualification standards on "frequency of trades."

CBA is not yet salvation or replacement for hitting your numbers, including volume of trades, days per week with executed trades, and average holding periods. But we think CBA can save the day on TTS when the frequency of transactions comes up a little short. Remember that an enormous Section 475 MTM ordinary loss is contingent on having TTS, so it's often worth defending.

CBA can plug holes in the frequency of trades. Suppose a trader has transactions three days a week instead of four. If that trader can establish CBA and argue the appeals or tax court correctly, the trader might win the case for TTS.

Assaderaghi, Nelson, Endicott, and other traders in the tax court have not yet adequately raised our CBA argument. Our research found that the IRS inappropriately adopted "frequency of trades" as its gold standard after the landmark trader case Paoli vs. Commissioner (1991). That's the nature of tax court case law: The IRS keeps making arguments based on prior cases, and case law takes on a life of its own. What went wrong for traders here? Paoli tried to cheat the IRS and tax court by claiming he was a full-time business trader, but he only had a handful of trades in one month during the year. His attempt was a fiasco. The tax court rightfully said we need a way to verify a wild statement by a taxpayer and prove his activity. Hence, the court turned to the frequency of trades argument to check on CBA but not to replace it. Other businesses don't have to go through the frequency of business standards either — the IRS presumes they have CBA.

The IRS conveniently overlooked this vital distinction, elevating "frequency of trades" as the standard that counts most in its audit manuals. But this is wrong because CBA still trumps the frequency of trades, which is meant to be a backup test only.

Consider a hotel analogy: A guest checks in on Monday and checks out on Saturday, using the front desk execution for two days that week. But the hotel staff serviced that guest for six days. Most TTS traders service open trades.

Impress the IRS with your CBA. Many traders work every day of the week, conducting extensive research, backtesting, writing code, making unexecuted trades, demo trading, learning new areas, making live trades, and handling administration, accounting, IT, and much more. During a tax exam, the amount of work involved, the sophisticated level of technology used, and the time spent on research and administration often impress the IRS. CBA is not hard to prove for most active traders.

If a trader establishes CBA, the court should not have the right to overturn that business treatment by arguing a trader falls a tiny bit short on some of its often-quoted tax court case standards.

Be prepared to be a guinea pig in arguing for CBA in tax court and ensure it's worth your while regarding outcome vs. cost.

HISTORY OF TTS AND SECTION 475

In 1997, Congress recognized TTS traders as a separate and respected tax class and expanded Section 475 mark-to-market accounting (MTM, ordinary gain or loss treatment) from dealers to TTS traders. As a result, some IRS agents confuse traders with dealers in exams.

Congress added the new Section 475(f) for "traders in securities" and "traders in commodities." Section 475(f) is recommended for many securities TTS traders but not generally commodities/futures traders because the latter prefer to keep the lower tax rates of Section 1256 60/40 capital gains tax rates. While Section 475(f) was enacted over 25 years ago, the IRS has failed to sufficiently clarify these tax laws, making life unduly difficult for traders and their accountants. The IRS did expand Publication 550 to include a new Chapter 4, "Special Rules for Traders" (available at www.irs.gov), but it speaks in generalities.

By failing to create clear statutory law on eligibility for TTS, the IRS is leaving the matter to tax-court judges to write case law. The IRS appears to be winning this game because its agents depict unsettled law as settled law and scare taxpayers into conceding TTS when they rightfully used it on their tax returns.

A few recent IRS tax court victories set a bad precedent for all non-hyperactive traders, especially part-time and money-losing traders. Familiarize yourself with these cases so you don't make the same mistakes.

Chapter 12

Proprietary Trading

Proprietary traders significantly differ from retail traders and have special tax compliance needs. They don't trade their capital. They trade the firm's capital, usually accessed from a sub-trading account. A prop trader becomes associated with a prop-trading firm either as an LLC member (Schedule K-1) or an independent contractor (1099-NEC).

If you fall in the prop trader category, here's what you need to know.

INDEPENDENT CONTRACTORS

Profitable independent contractor (IC) proprietary traders receive a Form 1099-NEC for "non-employee compensation." Sole proprietors use a Schedule C to report this fee revenue and deduct their business expenses, including home office deductions if they qualify. Schedule C net income is subject to federal and state income taxes.

That net income is "earned income" subject to the self-employment (SE) tax. The SE tax rate is 15.3% of the social security base amount of $160,200 for 2023 and $168,600 for 2024. The Medicare portion of SE tax is 2.9%, unlimited. When SEI exceeds the ACA AGI thresholds of $250,000 (married) and $200,000 (single), an additional 0.9% surtax matches the ACA net investment tax rate of 3.8%.

Firms don't issue 1099-NEC to IC traders with losses since they don't pay those traders a fee. Losing IC traders are still working, so they can file a Schedule C, which reports expenses only, including lost deposits.

What's the difference tax-wise between retail traders and IC prop traders? Retail trading gains aren't subject to the SE tax. IC prop traders have earned income, enabling them to contribute to tax-deductible retirement plans and deduct health insurance premiums. A retail trader with TTS needs to form an S-Corp to create compensation for these employee deductions.

IC prop traders may also trigger local taxes on earned income, like New York City's 4% Unincorporated Business Tax (UBT) tax. Retail TTS traders are subject to ACA 3.8% Net Investment Tax (NIT) on net investment income (NII) if they exceed the ACA thresholds. The main difference between SE and NIT is the Social Security tax in SE tax.

Some prop-trading firms may allow the IC trader to form a single-member LLC with an S-Corp election, so the trader may be able to reduce SE taxes by up to 50-75%.

SOME PROP TRADERS UNDERREPORT INCOME

Reinvested earnings are taxable income: Prop traders generate trading gains on their sub-trading account. At the end of the month, the firm gives them a choice: Request a fee payment (distribution of earnings) or reinvest the income in their sub-trading account.

Some prop firms only include fee payments on Form 1099-NEC. They don't account for reinvested earnings. That's a problem: In this scenario, reinvested earnings constitute "constructive receipt of income," which should be reportable income. These prop traders are likely under-reporting income since many will inadvertently or purposely overlook reporting reinvested earnings on Schedule C. Taxpayers are responsible for reporting all income on their tax return, even if the income is not reported on a 1099. (Read our blog, Some Proprietary Traders Under Report Income, https://tinyurl.com/gtt-under-report.)

ISSUES FOR LLC MEMBERS WITH K-1

LLC prop traders don't have earned income reported on their Schedule K-1s, so they save SE tax. Conversely, these prop traders can't contribute to a retirement plan or deduct self-employed health insurance premiums in connection with that unearned income.

Trading gains on Schedule K-1 are considered NII under ACA NIT. (Read about ACA taxes in Chapter 15.)

Prop trading firms report activity on a Form 1065 partnership tax return. Schedule K-1 reports the LLC member's share of the firm's trading gains and expenses — in summary format.

Schedule K-1, Box 1 is for ordinary income or loss. Most prop trading firms elect Section 475 MTM for securities, so the income is considered ordinary. Other firms pass through capital gains and losses on Section 1256 futures. The firm qualifies for TTS on the entity level and gives it to you on the K-1 with business expense treatment.

Prop firms prepare partnership tax returns since S-Corps do not allow special allocations to different ownership classes. Special allocations are fundamental to prop trading firms, as prop traders are treated differently from the principal owners. The IRS does not want trading partnerships to pay guaranteed payments to partners.

PROP TRADER EXPENSES

Like retail traders, many prop traders have trading expenses charged by the firm. The LLC members' Schedule K-1s ordinary income box deducts those expenses.

Some prop-trading firms have an "accountable reimbursement plan." If your firm doesn't have such a plan, you might be able to deduct your trading business expenses outside the firm, including your home office expenses, as "unreimbursed partnership expenses" (UPE). Schedule K-1 ordinary income is reported on Schedule E in the active column, as it's not a passive activity under the "trading rule" in Section 469. UPE is deducted in that same area on Schedule E on the following line under the Schedule K-1 ordinary income or loss. Most of the home office deduction requires income.

Trading expenses from a prop trading firm K-1 can reduce SEI or net investment income — that's good if you owe SE or NIT taxes, even if related to other activities.

TRADING LOSSES

Most prop trading firms take all trading losses at the principal's level. Firms only pay IC traders when they reach new high net profits, a concept used in investment management. With LLC-member prop traders, the Class-A member (company management) also takes losses on their K-1 and doesn't report ordinary income to the prop trader until they make new high net profits. If you have allocated trading losses on your Schedule K-1, ensure you have a sufficient basis (equity or debt basis) to take the loss on your current tax return. If you have no basis, the loss is suspended and will carry forward to subsequent tax years.

DEDUCTING LOST DEPOSITS

A fundamental tax issue prop traders face is when to deduct deposits lost within the firm. If you incur a trading loss, the firm may deduct it from the owner/manager's K-1, even if they use your deposit to cover the loss. How can you expense the lost deposit on your tax returns?

For an IC trader, Form 1099-NEC does not reflect their lost deposits. When realizing the loss, the IC trader can deduct a bad debt on Schedule C as a business expense. The deposit is forfeited when the trader must replenish it due to trading losses or if the trader must leave the firm and the firm doesn't repay the deposit. (If the trader is making money and still has that deposit, there's no loss-recognition event.)

These are deposits, not capital contributions, as LLC members.

If an LLC-member prop trader has a lost deposit, they deduct it as UPE on Schedule E.

For IC traders who spent $10,000 on education before becoming a prop trader in an education/prop trading hybrid firm (before acceptance as a prop trader), that money is considered pre-business education and is not deductible. Alternatively, consider capitalizing a portion as Section 195 business startup costs.

If they reclassify part of the $10,000 as a deposit and subsequently lose it, treat it as a deposit loss. Or, if they reclassify some of the education to post-business education (i.e., they start prop trading and take some classes afterward), they may have a business education expense.

Some IC prop traders never get paid and don't receive a 1099-NEC. Can they deduct post-business education or a deposit loss? If they work as a prop trader, they might be able to.

QBI DEDUCTION

Proprietary traders might be eligible for TCJA's 20% deduction on qualified business income (QBI). Independent contractor prop traders may file a Schedule C or S-Corp tax return with revenue for trading services. Net income after expenses constitutes QBI, providing the prop trading firm is based in the U.S. Consulting is a "specified service trade or business" (SSTB) activity.

LLC member prop traders might also be eligible for the QBI deduction, providing the prop trading firm elected Section 475 ordinary income. The Schedule K-1 special allocation should include ordinary income. QBI excludes capital gains and losses. (See more on the QBI deduction in chapters 7 and 17.)

Chapter 13

Investment Management

Investment managers trade money belonging to investors. As you can imagine, handling other people's money is serious business. Therefore, many investor-protection laws and regulations on securities, commodities, and forex exist. The investment manager may need various licenses and register with the regulator.

SEPARATELY MANAGED ACCOUNT OR HEDGE FUND?

Investment managers handle two types of investors: separately managed accounts (SMAs) and hedge funds (commodity or forex pools). In an SMA, the client maintains a retail customer account, granting trading power to the investment manager. In a hedge fund, the investor pools their money for an equity interest in the fund, receiving an annual Schedule K-1 for their income and expense allocation. It's different with offshore hedge funds.

There are essential differences in tax treatment. SMAs cannot claim trader tax status (TTS) because the investment manager is responsible for the trading, not the investor. (The investment manager doesn't have TTS but has business treatment from providing investment management services.) The investor can't elect and use Section 475 MTM without TTS.

The 2017 Tax Cuts and Jobs Act (TCJA) suspended "certain miscellaneous itemized deductions subject to the 2% floor," including investment fees and expenses. TCJA disenfranchises SMA investors from deducting management and incentive fees. Hedge funds use carried interest, a profit-allocation provision, to convert incentive fees into a reduction of capital gains. (See New Tax Law Favors Hedge Funds Over Managed Accounts, https://tinyurl.com/gtt-hedge-funds.)

TCJA introduced a business interest expense limitation if gross receipts (net trading gains) exceed $25 million per year.

The manager's profit allocation has other tax advantages: The carried-interest share of capital gains or Section 475 ordinary income is exempt from payroll taxes, whereas advisory fees receive earned income treatment subject to payroll taxes (Social Security and Medicare).

With a hedge fund structure, the investment manager is generally an owner/trader of the fund and brings TTS to the entity level. A TTS hedge fund deducts management and incentive fees as a business expense on the partnership tax return.

In an SMA, the investor deals with accounting (including complex trade accounting on securities), not the investment manager. In a hedge fund, the investment manager is responsible for complex investor-level accounting. The fund sends investors a Schedule K-1 that is easier to input into tax returns.

TAX TREATMENT ELECTIONS

Hedge funds can make different tax treatment elections, but making them on time is essential. In some cases, these tax elections should be contemplated in the development process and included in the private placement memorandum. For example, investors with significant capital loss carryovers may search for hedge funds that will generate capital gains rather than Section 475 MTM ordinary income on securities or Section 988 ordinary income on forex. A hedge fund and SMA account owner can elect capital gains treatment on forex trading. Taxpayers must file the Section 988 forex capital gains election internally contemporaneously. (More on forex in Chapter 3.)

Most investors benefit from TTS, so if your fund qualifies, claiming it might be a good idea. TTS allows advisors and investors to treat business expenses without passive loss activity limitations. (One exception: non-active owners report investment interest expense as itemized deductions.) That means investors get the full benefit of advisory fees paid "above the line" (from gross income) rather than face TCJA-suspended investment fees and expense deductions.

Funds with TTS may elect Section 475 MTM on securities, which exempts them from wash-sale loss adjustments at year-end. Section 475 receives business ordinary loss treatment, avoiding capital loss limitations. Some managers skip a Section 475 election because they don't want the burden of contemporaneous segregation rules for investments vs. trading positions. They don't wish for MTM to apply at year-end so that they can defer capital gains to the next tax year(s). Otherwise, they would pass MTM income to investors who would likely want redemptions to pay taxes on the unrealized income while the manager has not sold those underlying shares yet. Some hedge funds have TTS and Section 475 MTM on one portfolio, and they properly segregate an investment portfolio without TTS, where they generate long-term capital gains. (Read Chapter 2 and our blog posts, Safeguard Use of Section 475 by Trading in an Entity, IRS Plays Havoc with Traders Misidentifying Investments, and IRS Warns Section 475 Traders, https://greentradertax.com/blog/archives.)

QBI DEDUCTION IN HEDGE FUNDS

Investment management companies are "specified service trade or businesses" (SSTB), and advisory fees from U.S. clients count as qualified business income (QBI). QBI also includes a "carried-interest" profit allocation of Section 475 income distributed to the management company. QBI excludes a carried interest of capital gains.

A hedge fund with TTS is like a TTS trading partnership for determining a QBI deduction. Hedge fund expenses are negative QBI, and Section 475 income is positive QBI. Some hedge fund accountants disagree based on their interpretation of Section 864(b). For more information on QBI, see Chapters 7 and 17. Hedge funds that don't elect 475 are not concerned with QBI issues.

CARRIED-INTEREST TAX BREAK

Hedge funds can use the carried-interest tax break, but separately managed accounts (SMAs) cannot. Suppose the fund's operating agreement includes carried interest. In that case, the partnership K-1 allocates a share of each item of income — let's say 20% — in place of the fund paying an outside advisor an incentive fee. Generally, the general partner and investors receive tax breaks with carried interest. The advisor gets a share of lower tax rates on 60/40 (futures) or long-term capital gains and avoids payroll tax on earned income, and the investor avoids suspended investment expense treatment.

Attorneys can arrange carried interest in offshore funds with a mini-master fund structure. There are other nuances in connection with the self-employment tax and the ACA 3.8% Medicare tax on unearned income (the investment income).

CARRIED INTEREST IS GOOD FOR INVESTORS

Investors are stuck with suspended investment-expense treatment and investment-interest-expense limitations for expenses that pass through an investment partnership. The most significant investment expense is often advisory fees paid to the investment manager.

Carried interest reclassifies incentive fees from suspended investment expenses into reduced capital gains, equivalent to a deduction from gross income and net investment income.

For example, a hedge fund investor with a $100,000 capital gain has a net gain of $80,000 after applying the 20% carried-interest provision. Without carried interest, the capital gain would be $100,000, and the investor would have a suspended investment expense deduction for regular tax and ACA's 3.8% net investment tax.

CARRIED-INTEREST MODIFIED IN TCJA

TCJA modified the carried interest tax break for investment managers in investment partnerships, lengthening their holding period on profit allocation of long-term capital gains (LTCG) to three years from one year. If the manager also invests capital in the investment partnership, they have LTCG after one year on that interest. The three-year rule only applies to the investment manager's profit allocation — carried interest. Investors still have LTCG based on one year. Investment partnerships include hedge funds, commodity pools, and private equity funds. Many hedge funds don't hold securities for over three years, whereas private equity and venture capital funds do.

Carried interest in Section 1256 lower 60/40 capital gains still works.

The 2023 Inflation Reduction Act dropped proposed changes to the taxation of carried interest, including lengthening the holding period to five years from three.

BUSINESS INTEREST EXPENSE LIMITATION

More considerable hedge funds might be subject to TCJA's business interest limitation calculated on Form 8990 Limitation on Business Interest Expense Under Section 163(j). The threshold is gross receipts over $26 million annually, equating to a trading company's net trading gains. Learn more about the business interest expense limitation in Chapters 7 and 17.

S-CORP TAX REDUCTION STRATEGY

Although investment managers can't use profit-allocation clauses on SMAs, they can use the S-Corp SE tax reduction loophole to reduce social security (FICA) and Medicare taxes on earned income. Managed accounts pay advisory fees, which include management and incentive fees, whereas funds using profit allocation clauses only pay management fees.

In an LLC management company filing a partnership tax return, earned income passes through to the LLC owners as SEI subject to SE tax unless an owner is passive.

Investment managers can only use profit allocation with investment funds because only partners can share special allocations of underlying income. Special allocations are helpful on fund partnership tax filings but not with S-Corp tax returns since they reverse (taint) S-Corp elections. The IRS only allows S-Corps to have one class of stock and insists on equal ownership treatment.

That makes S-Corp elections a wise choice for management companies focused on reducing the SE tax on underlying advisory fee earned income. Conversely, partnership tax returns are better for investment funds focused on carried-interest tax breaks using special allocations. There is generally no underlying income subject to the SE tax, anyway.

An existing LLC or C-Corp can file an S-Corp election (Form 2553) by March 15 of the current tax year. Many states accept the federal election, but some require a state election. The IRS has relief for late S-Corp elections but requires a perjury statement saying you intended to elect it on time.

The IRS knows of this S-Corp SE tax reduction strategy, so it insists owners pay themselves "reasonable compensation." Industry practice is 25-50% of net income. The remaining percentage is free of payroll tax or SE tax. The IRS is turning up the heat on S-Corps with tax exams and forcing this type of officer's compensation. The IRS has a computer program to look for reasonable "compensation of officers" on Form 1120S S-Corp tax returns. Recent case law favors the IRS, so don't skip this requirement. A TTS S-Corp has underlying unearned income, so it's not subject to reasonable compensation guidelines. Learn more about entities for traders and investment managers in Chapter 7, including many tips on using an S-Corp.

C-CORPS WITH A 21% TAX RATE

TCJA significantly reduced the C-Corp tax rate to a 21% flat rate, commencing in 2018. Investment managers in corporate-tax-free states may prefer a C-Corp structure for their management company. (See how TCJA impacts entity choices in Chapters 7 and 17.)

Chapter 14

International Tax

U.S. traders move abroad; others make international investments and nonresident aliens invest in the U.S. How are their taxes handled?

U.S. RESIDENT TRADERS LIVING ABROAD

U.S. tax residents are liable for federal tax on worldwide income whether they live in the U.S. or a foreign country. A U.S. tax resident has U.S. citizenship or a permanent resident card (green card). If you qualify for "bona fide" or "physical residence" abroad, which is living abroad for an entire tax year, try to arrange Section 911 "foreign earned income" benefits on Form 2555. Avoid the potential double taxation of paying tax in both a foreign country and the U.S. by availing yourself of foreign tax credits reported on Form 1116. If you live in a country with higher taxes than the U.S., skipping the Section 911 exclusion may make sense because creating officer compensation in a TTS S-Corp also causes some U.S. payroll taxes (FICA and Medicare). It might be better to go the foreign tax credit route.

The "foreign earned income exclusion" (FEIE) is $120,000 for 2023 and $126,500 for 2024, which the IRS raises yearly. There is also a housing allowance and a maximum amount (cap) per location. The problem for traders is that an IRS publication indicates that capital gains and trading gains are not "foreign earned income." Hence, they are likely unable to utilize Section 911 benefits unless they create officer compensation with a TTS S-Corp.

There is a solution: TTS traders with trader tax status can form an SMLLC with an S-Corp election to pay officer compensation, and that compensation is foreign earned income. Before committing to this solution, compare expected net income tax savings, minus payroll tax costs, vs. using a foreign tax credit.

The U.S. has tax treaties with many countries, and these agreements specify which country is entitled to collect tax on different types of items, like capital gains and retirement plan distributions. Cite a tax treaty provision to override a regular tax on Form 8833. It's important to note that taxpayers use tax treaty provisions to reduce tax liability; the IRS may not use them to increase a tax.

The 2017 Tax Cuts and Jobs Act (TCJA) changed corporate taxation from a worldwide tax regime to a territorial one. However, it did not convert citizen-based taxation to residence-based taxation for U.S. residents living and working abroad. Therefore, the law continues for foreign-earned income and housing allowance exclusions for U.S. residents abroad. TCJA suspended the moving expense deduction starting in 2018.

The IRS grants U.S. residents living abroad 60 days additional time for the income tax return or extension deadline — June 15 instead of April 15. They can file a Form 4868 extension by June 15 to extend their tax return to Oct. 15. One caveat: If you owe taxes, the IRS charges interest from April 15.

U.S. RESIDENT TRADERS WITH INTERNATIONAL BROKERAGE ACCOUNTS

Some traders living in the U.S. have a foreign brokerage account. It's complicated when traders open these accounts held in a foreign currency. Counterparties outside the U.S. do not issue Form 1099-Bs, and accounting is challenging. Many foreign banks and brokers report U.S. residents' account activity to the U.S. Treasury and IRS per FATCA. Traders should separate capital gains and losses, including currency appreciation or depreciation, from changes in currency values on cash balances.

Some foreign brokers encourage traders to form foreign entities to get access or set up an account. Look before you leap: Tax compliance for an international entity is significant, and traders have few to no tax advantages. Global tax compliance is complex, and there's a risk of messing up tax reporting. It's scarce to achieve material deferral on foreign income, and there are plenty of tax penalties for non-compliance. But there are good reasons to trade foreign markets. Get the right advice beforehand and ensure the motivation to do so is compelling.

Foreign countries may withhold income taxes on various types of portfolio income, and traders should review income and estate tax treaties for provisions that might apply. Traders with foreign withholding income on foreign transactions may be unable to use the foreign taxes as credits against their U.S. income tax liability. Tax law generally treats all trading gains as U.S. source income, even when generated on foreign exchanges. In this situation, you may claim the benefits of an income tax treaty (if available) to reduce foreign taxes.

Some U.S.-based brokers offer access to financial markets outside the U.S., and the broker maintains the account in U.S. dollars, making it more convenient for the taxpayer.

REPORT OF FOREIGN ACCOUNTS

U.S. residents with a foreign bank, brokerage, investment, and another type of account (including retirement and insurance in some cases) who meet reporting requirements must e-file FinCEN Form 114, Report of Foreign Bank and Financial Account (known previously as Foreign Bank Account Reports or "FBAR"). If your foreign bank and financial institution accounts combined are under $10,000 during the entire tax year, you fall under the threshold for filing FinCEN Form 114.

A law enacted on July 31, 2015, changed the due date from June 30 to April 15, starting with 2016 filings in 2017. Congress added an automatic six-month extension to Oct. 15 to coordinate FinCEN Form 114 with individual income tax returns.

Many taxpayers omitted foreign bank account reports when they should have filed them. Some didn't realize they had a filing requirement. Others had a financial interest in accounts offshore if they were foreign nationals before moving to the U.S. Some taxpayers gained the interest via marriage. Others may have international retirement or insurance accounts they never realized were subject to FBAR reporting.

The FBAR rule states "a financial interest in, signature authority or other authority over foreign financial accounts." Traders, executives of hedge funds, and other financial institutions and trustees typically have signature authority or other authority over foreign financial accounts triggering FinCEN 114 filings.

Most taxpayers owning foreign accounts reported their foreign income and were not trying to cheat the IRS by hiding it offshore. Because they reported foreign income correctly, many can file a late FinCEN 114 and avoid penalties. Otherwise, there is a highly complex and nuanced penalty regime concerning late or incorrect FBAR filings.

FOREIGN RETIREMENT PLANS

Don't assume international retirement plans are like U.S. pension plans with tax deferral on income until you take taxable distributions. For U.S. tax purposes, the IRS considers many international retirement plans taxable investment accounts because they aren't structured as qualified plans under Section 401 unless they qualify under Section 402(b) as an employee's trust established by an employer. While that seems unfair and counterintuitive to many, it's the rule and catches many unsuspecting taxpayers and accountants off guard. If Section 402(b) does not apply, you may have to pay a high Passive Foreign Investment Company (PFIC) tax. Include these retirement plans on the annual FinCEN Form 114 each year, whether or not the plan has deferral.

In October 2014, the IRS acknowledged and assisted with the tax-deferral problem in Canadian retirement plans. In Revenue Procedure 2014-55, the IRS repealed the need to file a tax election, meaning Canadian retirement plans automatically qualify for tax deferral. These rules are retroactive, so they abate (remove) back taxes, interest, and penalties. Filing Form 8891 (U.S. Information Return for Beneficiaries of Certain Canadian Registered Retirement Plans) is no longer needed. This relief does not apply to international retirement plans outside of Canada.

FOREIGN ASSETS REPORTED ON FORM 8938

Tax Form 8938 is akin to giving the IRS a heads-up regarding your international assets. It's not about reporting income and loss. The filing threshold for Form 8938 is materially higher than the FinCEN 114 threshold and even higher for Americans living out of the country. (See Form 8938 instructions.)

NONRESIDENT ALIENS ARE OPENING U.S. BROKERAGE ACCOUNTS

The U.S. stock markets have been stellar over the past decade, and many non-U.S. persons have accessed them from their home countries. Other foreign individuals and entities prefer to open U.S.-based brokerage accounts for lower commissions and better trading platforms.

In either case, the foreign individual or company is subject to U.S. tax withholding on U.S. dividends and other U.S. passive income. The default withholding tax rate is 30%, and income tax treaties provide lower rates, usually around 15% or less. U.S. brokers handle the tax withholding and pay those taxes to the IRS. The foreign investor does not have an obligation for U.S. tax compliance if U.S. brokers calculate and report their withholding correctly.

The critical point is that capital gains are not taxable in the U.S. if the nonresident alien does not spend more than 183 days per year in the U.S. Most active traders don't generate significant dividend income from U.S. companies. Hence, tax withholding is not a problem. Many get a foreign tax credit for U.S. tax withholding in their resident country.

Some nonresident aliens establish a spousal-member LLC in the U.S. and file a U.S. partnership tax return. The LLC/partnership opens a U.S.-based brokerage account as a domestic entity. The LLC files a W-9 with a U.S. tax identification number. The broker treats the U.S. LLC/partnership as a U.S. account, which means the broker does not handle the tax withholding on dividends and other passive income for the foreign owners of the LLC. Therefore, the nonresident alien owners must file a W-8BEN with the U.S. partnership. The U.S. partnership assumes responsibility for tax withholding on dividends and other portfolio income and payment of those taxes to the IRS on a timely basis. It's extra tax compliance work, but it's not too complicated.

U.S. estate tax might come into play. Estate tax treaties may exempt brokerage accounts for nonresident aliens or provide higher exemptions from the tax. U.S. partnership interests are likely not included in a nonresident alien's estate. Brokers are not responsible for estate tax compliance, so it's a tax matter for nonresident aliens and their tax advisors. Brokers require a conclusion of IRS estate proceedings before releasing assets from the deceased's account.

Nonresident alien U.S. income tax treatment. In this scenario, nonresident aliens are subject to U.S. tax withholding on U.S. companies' dividends and other "fixed or determinable, annual, or periodic" (FDAP) income. Per IRS Taxation of Nonresident Aliens (at www.irs.gov): "FDAP income is passive income such as interest, dividends, rents, or royalties. This income is taxed at a flat 30% rate unless a tax treaty specifies a lower rate."

Many countries have a tax treaty with the U.S. providing a 15% or lower withholding tax rate on FDAP income. Interest income on bonds and commercial paper issued by U.S. companies, the U.S. Treasury, and U.S. government agencies is generally exempt from U.S. tax withholding. However, it's reportable on Form 1042-S.

Nonresident alien individuals fill out W-8BEN (Certificate of Foreign Status of Beneficial Owner for United States Tax Withholding and Reporting) and furnish it to the broker. Don't overlook Part II to claim tax treaty benefits. The broker then withholds taxes on U.S.-source dividends and other FDAP income at the appropriate tax treaty rates, or 30% if there is no tax treaty, and pays those taxes to the IRS directly. As a withholding agent, the broker must report all U.S.-source FDAP to the IRS and the client on Form 1042-S. There are other types of W-8 forms, including W-8BEN-E (entities), W-8ECI (ECI from U.S. business), W-8EXP (foreign government or organization), and W-8IMY (foreign intermediary or branch).

However, treaties do not benefit income generated by a U.S. trade or business (termed "income effectively connected" or ECI). For example, a nonresident alien partner carrying on a U.S. business will likely generate ECI, leading to income tax liability at net, graduated rates.

Capital gains 183-day rule. If the nonresident alien spends more than 183 days in the U.S., they owe taxes on net U.S. source capital gains, even though they may not trigger U.S. residency under the substantial presence test. (U.S. residency is started with legal residence status or by meeting the substantial presence test. The IRS taxes U.S. residents on worldwide income.)

See IRS The Taxation of Capital Gains of Nonresident Alien Students, Scholars and Employees of Foreign Governments (at www.irs.gov):

"Nonresident alien students and scholars and alien employees of foreign governments and international organizations who, at the time of their arrival in the United States, intend to reside in the United States for longer than one year are subject to the 30 percent taxation on their capital gains during any tax year (usually a calendar year) in which they are present in the United States for 183 days or more unless a tax treaty provides for a lesser rate of taxation. These capital gains would be reported on page 4 (not page 1) of Form 1040NR and would not be reported on a Schedule D because they are being taxed at a flat rate of 30 percent or at a reduced flat rate under a tax treaty." (Learn more in my blog post, How to Save U.S. Taxes for Nonresident Aliens, https://tinyurl.com/gtt-nonresident-aliens, and Webinar recording, How Non-U.S. Residents Save U.S. Taxes on U.S. Brokerage Accounts, https://tinyurl.com/webinar-nonresident-aliens.)

FOREIGN ACCOUNT TAXPAYER COMPLIANCE ACT

Foreign Account Taxpayer Compliance Act (FATCA) regulations were enacted in July 2014. The IRS and U.S. Treasury are intimidating foreign banks into reporting their American clients — even in countries like Switzerland, known for bank secrecy.

FATCA penalizes foreign banks and brokers for not helping with tax compliance for U.S. citizens and residents. The FATCA rules are so demanding, tedious, and costly to comply with that many smaller foreign banks and brokers now refuse to do business with Americans; it's just not worth the burden and risk. Some brokers ask their U.S. clients to form offshore entities to navigate FATCA, but that often doesn't work and can be a huge problem for U.S. taxpayers. FATCA is highly controversial, and Congress may water it down in the future.

Some countries appreciate the reciprocal exchange of tax information.

FOREIGN-BASED FOREX BROKERS/BANKS

CFTC rules require foreign forex brokers and banks to be registered with the National Futures Association (NFA) and U.S. bank regulator, respectively, if they want to handle American retail customers. These CFTC rules limit allowable leverage to 50:1 on major and 20:1 on minor currencies. These CFTC rules don't apply to U.S. "eligible contract participants" (ECP) meeting those high net worth thresholds.

The NFA hedging rule requires "first in, first out" only, which disallows hedging or spread betting.

These U.S. rules have upset many forex traders with their trading programs, and they've considered all possible angles for working with offshore forex brokers or banks. CFTC rules don't apply directly to customers but rather to forex brokers. It might not be safe to do business with an unregistered foreign forex broker who might become subject to CFTC enforcement actions. Offshore companies don't help evade these rules, according to a CFTC enforcement attorney.

Chapter 15

ACA Net Investment Income Tax

The 2012 Patient Protection and Affordable Care Act (ACA) introduced the 3.8% Net Investment Income Tax (NIT) on upper-income individuals and trusts.

NET INVESTMENT INCOME TAX (NIT)

Initially called the ACA 3.8% Medicare surtax on unearned income, NIT affected upper-income taxpayers. It only applies to individuals with net investment income (NII) and modified adjusted gross income (AGI) exceeding $200,000 single, $250,000 married filing jointly, or $125,000 married filing separately. Congress did not index these ACA thresholds for inflation. (Modified AGI means U.S. residents abroad must add back any foreign earned income exclusion reported on Form 2555.) The tax also applies to irrevocable trusts (and estates) on the undistributed NII more than the dollar amount at which the highest tax bracket for trusts begins.

NET INVESTMENT INCOME

Notice the terms "investment income" and "unearned income." People who receive earned income from a job pay Social Security (on the Social Security base amount) and Medicare tax on their wages or self-employment income. Unearned income generally includes interest, dividends, rents, royalties, capital gains, and income/loss from passive and pass-through investment and trading companies. NIT also subjects this income to Medicare taxes, albeit at upper-income brackets. (Take a look at Form 8960 and the final IRS regulations.)

NII requires segregating different types of unearned income into three buckets:

- Portfolio income (includes interest, dividends, and annuity distributions), royalties (net of oil and gas depletion expenses), and rents (net of depreciation);
- Passive activity income and loss from pass-through entities and investment and trading companies;
- Capital gains net of capital losses.

NII excludes:

- Wages and self-employment income;
- Tax-free municipal bond interest income;
- IRA and qualified plan distributions;

- Income from the disposition of, or pass-through from, active (earned-income related) LLCs, partnerships, and S-corps;
- Capital gain received from the sale of your company (and you have been active in it);
- Income from rental real estate; and
- The "exclusion" portion of a capital gain on the sale of a primary residence. Include the taxable portion above the exclusion amount in NII.

NIT CALCULATIONS

Calculate NIT on whatever is lower: NII or the AGI amount over the threshold. Here's an example: A single taxpayer has $300,000 AGI, which is $100,000 over the $200,000 modified AGI threshold. NII is $125,000 after deducting expenses. (Trading business expenses on Schedule C or E offset self-employment income first and deduct any excess against NII.) Since NII is higher than the AGI amount over the threshold, NIT is calculated on the lower amount, or $100,000 in this example: 3.8% x $100,000 = $3,800 NIT on Form 8960. If the taxpayer had $75,000 NII, NIT would be calculated on the lower amount instead (3.8% x $75,000 = $2,850).

NII DEDUCTIONS

In 2018, TCJA suspended "certain miscellaneous itemized deductions subject to the 2% floor," including investment fees and expenses. The IRS removed those line items from Schedule A.

Section 1411 regulations for NIT require that a permissible deduction for NII must first be allowed elsewhere on an income tax return, and investment fees and expenses are no longer deductibles on Schedule A or otherwise. Therefore, it may be best not to deduct investment fees and expenses on Form 8960 in determining NII.

Form 8960 Part II, "Investment Expenses Allocable to Investment Income and Modifications," allows line-item deductions for investment-interest expenses; state, local, and foreign income taxes; and miscellaneous investment expenses.

GOOD NEWS ON TRADING LOSSES

The regulations state: "To minimize the inconsistencies between Chapter 1 and Section 1411 for traders, the final regulations assign all trading gains and trading losses to section 1411(c)(1)(A)(iii) (bucket 3). The final regulations also permit a taxpayer to deduct excess losses from the trading business of a Section 475 trader from other categories of income (other buckets). Part 5.C of this preamble describes the treatment of those excess losses."

Therefore, a Section 475 MTM trader who arbitrages securities trades against interest income has interest income in bucket #1 and securities trading gains and losses in bucket #3. It's possible to offset bucket #1 with net Section 475 MTM ordinary losses in bucket #3.

When applicable, a $3,000 capital loss and a passive-activity loss are allowed against other NII buckets. The NII components of NOL carryforwards may be used against different NII buckets, too. Capital loss carryovers offset current-year capital gains in the usual way for income and NIT.

MISCELLANEOUS

While the Medicare tax on earned income is 50% tax deductible, it's not deductible on unearned income. Additionally, traders with low income or losses probably appreciate help from ACA in obtaining Medicaid or subsidized health insurance on an exchange. If your income is higher than projected, you may have to pay back some of the exchange subsidies on Form 8962. If your income is less than projected, you may qualify for a premium tax credit on Form 8962.

Chapter 16

Short Selling

The essence of trading is buying and selling financial products for income. If you think the asset will rise in value, buy first and sell afterward — this is known as a "long position." If you want to speculate on declining value, borrow the security to sell it first and then buy it later to close the short position — this is "selling short." (There are other ways to speculate on market drops, like buying put options or inverse ETFs, both of which are long positions.)

There are two types of short sales: (1) a short sale and (2) a short sale against the box. Both involve borrowing securities from another account holder arranged by a broker.

CONSTRUCTIVE SALES ON APPRECIATED POSITIONS

In the old days, owners stored stock certificates in safe deposit boxes. They could borrow and sell securities, but not those stored in their box — hence the moniker, "short sale against the box." It became a popular tax shelter to defer capital gains taxes.

The Taxpayer Relief Act of 1997 mostly closed the deferral loophole by adding new Section 1259 Constructive Sales Treatment For Appreciated Financial Positions. Before these changes, a trader could own security A with a significant unrealized capital gain and short it against the box before year-end to economically freeze the capital gain but defer the realization of it until the following year. Exception: A trader can still achieve tax deferral on an open short against the box position at year-end if he buys to cover the open short position by Jan. 30 and leaves the long position available throughout the 60 days beginning on the date he closes the transaction. So, there is an economic risk.

An example from Pub. 550 Investment Income and Expenses, Short Sales: "On May 9, 2019, you bought 100 shares of Baker Corporation stock for $1,000. On Sept. 12, 2019, you sold short 100 shares of similar Baker stock for $1,600. You made no other transactions involving Baker stock for the rest of 2019 and the first 30 days of 2020. Your short sale is treated as a constructive sale of an appreciated financial position because a sale of your Baker stock on the date of the short sale would have resulted in a gain. You recognize a $600 short-term capital gain from the constructive sale, and your new holding period in the Baker stock begins on Sept. 12."

The constructive sale rules apply to substantially identical properties, which include equities, equity options (including put options), futures, and other contracts. For example, Apple's equity is substantially identical to Apple's call-and-put equity options. Traders use a bevy of financial products and may inadvertently trigger Section 1259 constructive sales. Report gains on constructive sales, not losses.

Brokers do not report constructive sales on appreciated positions on Form 1099-Bs. Traders need to make manual adjustments on Form 8949. We recommend using tax-compliant software or a service provider that uses tax-compliant software.

SHORT-TERM VS. LONG-TERM CAPITAL GAINS AND LOSSES

Most traders understand capital gains rules for long positions. For securities using the realization method, a position held for 12 months or less is a short-term capital gain or loss subject to marginal ordinary tax rates (up to 37% for 2023 and 2024). A position held for more than 12 months is a long-term capital gain with lower capital gains tax rates (up to 20% for 2023 and 2024).

According to Pub. 550, "As a general rule, you determine whether you have a short-term or long-term capital gain or loss on a short sale by the time you hold the property eventually delivered to the lender to close the short sale."

If you sell short without owning substantially identical property (stock or option) in your account, the holding period starts when you later buy the position to close the short sale. The holding period is one day, a short-term capital gain or loss. Most investors think selling short is the reverse of going long, and the holding period should start on the date you short the security — but that is not the case.

Holding period rules are complicated when you short against the box. Special anti-abuse regulations in Section 1233 prevent traders from converting short-term capital gains into long-term capital gains and long-term capital losses into short-term ones.

SPECIAL RULES IN IRS PUB 550

Gains and holding period. If you held the substantially identical property for one year or less on the date of the short sale, or if you acquired the substantially identical property after the short sale and by the date of closing the short sale, then:

- Rule 1. Your gain, if any, when you close the short sale is a short-term capital gain, and
- Rule 2. The holding period of the substantially identical property begins on the date of the closing of the short sale or the date of the sale of this property, whichever comes first.

Losses. If you held the substantially identical property for more than one year on the short sale date, the realized loss is a long-term capital loss, even if you had the property used to close the sale for one year or less. Certain losses on short sales of stock or securities are also subject to wash-sale treatment.

DIVIDENDS AND PAYMENTS IN LIEU OF DIVIDENDS

When traders borrow shares to sell short, they receive dividends that belong to the lender, the rightful owner of the equity shares. After the short seller gets these dividends, the broker uses collateral in the seller's account to remit a "payment in lieu of dividend" to the owner to make the lender square economically. However, some complications may lead to higher taxes.

DIVIDEND ISSUES FOR THE SHORT SELLER

If a short seller holds the position open for 45 days or less, add the payments in lieu of dividends to the cost basis of the short sale transaction on Form 8949 (realization method) or Form 4797 (Section 475 MTM method). Watch out for a capital loss limitation. If you hold the position for more than 45 days, payments in lieu of dividends are deductible as investment interest expense (reported on Form 4952). The current-year tax deduction is limited to net investment income, including portfolio income minus certain investment expenses, but not other expenses suspended as itemized deductions in TCJA. (See Form 4952 instructions.) Carryover disallowed investment interest expense to the subsequent tax year(s). With itemized deduction limitations, some short sellers are short on investment interest expense deductions. Traders with trader tax status (TTS) using Section 475 are unconcerned, as they have ordinary loss treatment. (If a short seller holds the sale open for more than 45 days in connection with a TTS business, payments in lieu of dividends are deductible as business expenses.)

DIVIDEND ISSUES FOR THE LENDER

When investors sign margin account agreements, few realize they authorize their broker to lend their shares to short sellers. Instead of issuing the account owner (lender) a Form 1099-DIV, which may include ordinary and qualified dividends, the broker issues a Form 1099-MISC or similar statement for "other income." The lender forgoes the qualified dividends tax break on common stock held for at least 60 days. Lower capital gains rates apply on qualified dividends.

Lenders report this substitute dividend payment as "other income" on 2023 Schedule 1 (Form 1040). Don't overlook including substitute dividends in investment income entered on Form 4952 used to limit investment interest expense. Some brokers offer to compensate lenders for losing the qualified dividend rate. Institutional or large stock lenders may earn credit interest on lending out their shares. Include substitute dividend income in net investment income for the ACA net investment tax.

STOCK BORROW FEES AND LOAN PREMIUMS

Short selling is not free; a trader needs a broker to arrange a stock loan. Brokers charge short sellers "stock borrow fees" or "loan premiums." Tax research indicates these payments are "fees for the temporary use of property." Watch out: Many brokers refer to stock borrow fees as "interest expense," which confuses short sellers and their accountants.

Although it's uncertain in the tax code, there might be a rationale for investors to deduct stock borrow fees as "other itemized deductions" on line 16 of Schedule A (itemized deductions). The code seems to include it, but Schedule A instructions do not. Consult a tax professional.

Stock borrow fees are business expenses when the taxpayer has TTS.

Stock borrow fees are not interest expenses, so investors can't include them in those deductions.

SUPPORT FOR THIS TAX POSITION

According to New York City tax attorney Roger D. Lorence: "Short sale expenses (stock borrow fees) are not investment interest expense. There must be a valid interest-bearing obligation under state or federal law to support any interest deduction. (See Stroud v. U.S.) The IRS has ruled that short sales do not give rise to an interest-bearing indebtedness (*Revenue Ruling 95-8, 1995-1 CB 107*). Rather, the short sale borrower is liable under state law to return the borrowed stock and pay fees, but this is not an interest expense. Therefore, short sales do not give rise to Section 514 UBIT (no debt-financed property), the specific code section in the ruling. The revenue ruling is based on Deputy v. du Pont. The du Pont case applies by analogy because no interest expense can be generated in a short sale."

EASY VS. HARD TO BORROW FEES

Very liquid securities are labeled "easy to borrow." Many brokers charge small fees to short sellers for lending out those shares. Non-liquid securities are "hard to borrow," so brokers charge higher fees; most publish those rates with sample calculations on their websites. Hard-to-borrow fee rates rise as demand for shorting increases. A few brokers specialize in finding these stocks and charge up-front borrow fees and hard-to-borrow fees.

SOME BROKERS CONFLATE STOCK BORROW FEES WITH INTEREST EXPENSES

There is a lack of clarity in separating stock borrow fees from interest expenses. The distinction matters since borrow fees *might be* "other itemized deductions," whereas interest is an investment interest expense.

I wonder if some brokers prefer using the term interest expense since customers may find that more logical with borrowing shares under securities lending agreements. Customers may also object to paying significant fees.

For example, one leading online broker called the "interest rate charged on borrowed shares" a "fee rate" and also "net short stock interest." This broker does not report the fees on Form 1099.

Other online brokers mention interest on shorted shares as a "fee rate." They reported "miscellaneous non-reportable deductions" on Form 1099.

One of the largest online brokers states on its website: "When you borrow the shares, you pay interest to the brokerage house for this loan, and the harder the shares are to find, the higher the interest rate." We called customer support, and a support person admitted it was a stock-borrowing fee, not an interest expense.

There needs to be more clarity in separating stock borrow fees from interest expenses.

ACTIVE TRADERS USING SECTION 475 HAVE IT EASIER

Active traders qualifying for TTS with a Section 475 MTM election have an easier time reporting short-sale trades and related expenses, and they maximize tax advantages. They are unaffected by special rules for short sales relating to constructive sales on appreciated positions and holding period rules. (Section 475 exempts traders from the $3,000 capital loss limitation against other income, wash-sale losses, and short-sale adjustments.)

Section 475 allows traders to impute sales at year-end on open positions. That negates the need for "constructive sales on appreciated positions" from selling short against the box. Short- vs. long-term holding periods are not an issue with Section 475. TTS unlocks business expense treatment, so expenses related to selling short (including stock borrow fees and interest expenses) are deductible from gross income. Sole proprietors use Schedule C for reporting business expenses.

Chapter 17

Tax Cuts and Jobs Act

The 2017 Tax Cuts and Jobs Act (TCJA) impacted investors, traders, and individuals positively and negatively, beginning in the tax year 2018. In this chapter, we explore TCJA's impact on these groups.

The 2020 pandemic relief CARES Act overrode many TCJA rules for 2018, 2019, and 2020, and TCJA returned in force for 2021.

QUALIFIED BUSINESS INCOME DEDUCTION

TCJA introduced a new tax deduction for pass-through businesses, including sole proprietors, partnerships, and S-Corps. Subject to haircuts and limitations, a pass-through business could be eligible for a 20% deduction on qualified business income (QBI).

Traders eligible for TTS are a "specified service trade or business" (SSTB) activity, which means if their taxable income is above an income cap, they won't receive a QBI deduction. The taxable income (TI) cap is $464,200/$232,100 (married/other taxpayers) for 2023 and $483,900/$241,950 (married/other taxpayers) for 2024. The phase-out range below the cap is $100,000/$50,000 (married/other taxpayers), in which the QBI deduction phases out for SSTB. The W-2 wage and property basis limitations apply within the phase-out range. Investment managers are also SSTB.

QBI for traders includes Section 475 ordinary income and loss and trading business expenses. QBI excludes capital gains and losses, Section 988 forex ordinary income or loss, dividends, and interest income.

TCJA favors non-service businesses, which are not subject to an income cap. The W-2 wage and property basis limitations apply above the TI threshold of $364,200/$182,100 (married/other taxpayers) for 2023 and $383,900/$191,950 (married/other taxpayers) for 2024. The IRS adjusts the annual TI threshold for inflation each year.

Sole proprietor TTS traders cannot pay themselves wages and likely cannot use the phase-out range. (See more on QBI in chapter 9.)

EXCESS BUSINESS LOSSES AND NET OPERATING LOSSES

TCJA introduced the "excess business loss" (EBL) limitation and revised the net operating loss (NOL) rules. TTS traders with Section 475 MTM, ordinary loss treatment, can generate EBL and NOL carryforwards. TTS traders without 475 have capital loss limitations.

EBL can offset all types of income on a joint or single filing, whereas capital losses only offset capital gains. Plus, business expenses and ordinary trading losses comprise an NOL carryforward. Whether you are a trader or not in a carryforward year doesn't matter. Business ordinary trading loss treatment is the most significant contributor to federal and state tax refunds for traders.

TCJA repealed the two-year NOL carryback, except for certain farming losses and casualty and disaster insurance companies. TCJA carries forward NOLs indefinitely (20 years before the TCJA changes), and the deduction of NOLs is limited to 80% of the subsequent year's taxable income.

TCJA's 2018 EBL limitation was $500,000 for married and $250,000 for other taxpayers. Add the losses above the EBL to an NOL carryforward.

The inflation-adjusted EBL threshold for 2023 is $578,000 (for married)/$289,000 (for other taxpayers), and the 2024 EBL is $610,000 (for married)/$305,000 (for other taxpayers).

The 2020 CARES Act for COVID-19 relief suspended TCJA's EBL rules for 2018, 2019, and 2020 and allowed five-year NOL carrybacks. Taxpayers could recalculate their NOLs without the EBL limitation and file an NOL carryback refund claim. For example, they could carry back a 2020 NOL to 2015 and an unused NOL to 2016 and subsequent years. TCJA's NOL and EBL rules apply again in 2021 through 2025. Other recent tax acts extended EBL further to 2028. (See examples of EBL and NOL for Chapter 9.)

INVESTORS

TCJA suspends "certain miscellaneous itemized deductions that are subject to the 2% floor." These include investment fees and certain investment expenses, unreimbursed employee business expenses (job expenses), and tax compliance fees for non-business taxpayers.

Suspended investment expenses include trading expenses when the trader is not eligible for trader tax status (TTS) and investment advisory fees and costs paid to investment managers. Investment-interest expenses remain an itemized deduction. TTS traders have business expense treatment, so qualification for that status is essential to receive a tax benefit for trading-related expenses.

Suspended investment expenses are also not deductible from ACA's net investment income for net investment tax.

Family offices. A family office (FO) is a wealthy family with substantial investments across multiple asset classes. The FO hires staff, leases office space, and purchases computers and other fixed assets for its investment operations. An FO produces investment income, and most operating costs are investment expenses. Potentially losing the investment expense deduction comes as a shock to them. Some FOs evaluate which activities might qualify for business expense treatment to convert non-deductible investment expenses into business deductions from gross income. Some FOs investing in securities and Section 1256 contracts might ring-fence an active trading program into a separate TTS entity for business expenses. Some are not natural TTS traders, so that will be a challenge. Other FOs invest in rental real estate and venture capital, which might have business expense treatment. The goal is to allocate general and administrative expenses to business expenses. Some family offices have outside clients other than family members, and their management company passes IRS muster for business expense treatment.

A trader without TTS cannot merely form a dual-entity structure, including an investment partnership and S-Corp management company, and expect the management company to be a family office with business expense treatment. It won't work because the family manages their own money and has no outside clients. (See my blog, How to Avoid IRS Challenge on Your Family Office, https://tinyurl.com/gtt-family.)

Investment interest expenses. TCJA did not suspend or modify investment interest expense on Schedule A. Investment interest expense remains deductible up to the extent of investment income. Carry over the excess to the subsequent tax year.

Business interest expense modified. On Nov 26, 2018, the IRS and Treasury issued proposed regulations (REG-106089-18) for TCJA's new business interest limitation in Section 163(j). The IRS released a new tax Form 8990. Business interest expense is limited to 30% of adjusted taxable income, business interest income, and floor plan financing interest. Carry over the excess amount to subsequent tax years.

TTS traders deduct business interest expenses from gross income. Investors have investment-interest expense treatment, an itemized deduction limited to investment income, carrying over the excess to the following tax years.

The proposed regulation stated, "A small business taxpayer, other than a tax shelter, is not subject to this Section 163(j) limitation if the taxpayer's average annual gross receipts are $25 million or less for the three taxable years immediately preceding the current year."

When TCJA passed, we figured most TTS traders wouldn't have a business interest limitation because they wouldn't exceed $25 million per year in net trading gains — the equivalent of gross receipts for a TTS trader. More substantial TTS hedge funds certainly could reach that threshold.

After seeing the proposed regulations and reading what other tax writers had to say about it, we wondered if the IRS might seek to treat trading proceeds as gross receipts. That would snag many retail TTS traders. For example, a TTS trader with gross trading proceeds over $25 million and a net trading loss would have zero business expenses after the 30% income limitation.

However, the gross receipts test should look to net trading gains, not gross proceeds from the sale of capital assets. TTS traders don't have gross receipts from business operations. TTS traders use Section 162 for business expenses only and capital gains and losses or Section 475 for ordinary income or loss on the sale of capital assets.

Section 163(j) says to use the definition of "gross receipts" contained in Section 448, and the code does not include gross proceeds from the sale of securities. TCJA law and Section 163(j) regs do not include trading proceeds in gross receipts. In all other ways that we have addressed gross receipts before on the federal or state level, we have used net trading gains as gross margin, which corresponds with gross receipts.

The answer is in Treasury Reg. 1.448-1T(f)(2)(iv)(A), which supports our view that net trading gains equate to gross receipts for a TTS trader: "Gross receipts are not reduced by the cost of goods sold or by the cost of property sold if such property is described in section 1221(1), (3), (4) or (5). With respect to sales of capital assets as defined in section 1221, or sales of property described in 1221(2) (relating to property used in a trade or business), gross receipts shall be reduced by the taxpayer's adjusted basis in such property."

Active owners in a TTS hedge fund have business interest expenses; non-active owners have an investment interest expense. Section 163(j) applies to the partnership level.

Carried interest modified. TCJA modified the carried interest tax break for investment managers in investment partnerships, lengthening their holding period on profit allocation of long-term capital gains (LTCG) to three years from one year. If the manager also invests capital in the investment partnership, after one year, they have LTCG on that interest. The three-year rule only applies to the investment manager's profit allocation — carried interest. Investors still have LTCG based on one year. Investment partnerships include hedge funds, commodity pools, and private equity funds. Many hedge funds don't hold securities for over three years, whereas private equity and venture capital funds do.

Investors also benefit from carried interest in investment partnerships. Had the new tax law repealed carried interest outright, investment partnerships without TTS would be stuck passing investment advisory fees (incentive fees) through on Schedule K-1 as suspended investment fees and expenses. Carried interest fixes that: The partnership allocates capital gains to the investment manager instead of paying incentive fees. The investor winds up with a lower capital gain than a higher capital gain coupled with a suspended investment expense. For example, if the investor's share of net income is $80,000, they are happy to report $80,000 as a net capital gain. Without carried interest, the investor would report a $100,000 capital gain and have a $20,000 (20%) suspended investment fee.

Long-term capital gains rates retained. TCJA maintained the LTCG rates of 0%, 15%, and 20%. LTCG rates apply if an investor holds a security for more than 12 months before the sale or exchange. TCJA did not change the minor $3,000 capital loss limitation against other income or capital loss carryovers to subsequent tax years. TCJA also retained LTCG rates on qualified dividends.

60/40 capital gains rates retained. The 60/40 capital gains rates on Section 1256 contracts are intact, and TCJA did not change the Section 1256 loss carryback election. At the maximum tax bracket, the blended 60/40 rate is 26.8% — 10.2% lower than the top ordinary rate of 37%.

Wash-sale loss rules and Section 475. TCJA did not address wash-sale loss rules for securities. (For more on this lingering issue, see Chapter 4.) TCJA did not change Section 475 MTM ordinary income or loss. It did not change the tax treatment for various financial products, including spot forex in Section 988, ETFs, ETNs, volatility options, precious metals, swap contracts, foreign futures, and cryptocurrencies.

C-CORPS

When considering TCJA, traders shouldn't focus solely on the federal 21% flat tax rate on the C-Corp level. There are plenty of other taxes, including capital gains taxes on qualified dividends, corporate taxes in 44 states, and accumulated earnings tax assessed on excess retained earnings.

Double taxation occurs with capital gains taxes on the individual level when a C-Corp pays qualified dividends to the owner. If an owner avoids paying sufficient qualified dividends, the IRS can assess a 20% accumulated earnings tax (AET). It's a fallacy that owners cannot retain all earnings inside the C-Corp. Traders face difficulties creating a war chest plan to justify accumulated earnings and profits. A C-Corp investment company cannot retain earnings and profits without triggering AET. (See How to Decide if a C-Corp is Right for You, https://tinyurl.com/c-corp-trading.)

INDIVIDUALS

The individual tax changes are temporary through 2025, which applies to most provisions, including suspending certain investment expenses. Recent tax laws expanded the excess business loss (EBL) limitation to 2028.

TCJA enacted changes for individuals. The highlights for 2018 limits include the following:

- Lower tax rates in all seven brackets to 10%, 12%, 22%, 24%, 32%, 35%, and 37%; four tax brackets for estates and trusts: 10%, 24%, 35%, and 37%;
- Standard deduction raised to $24,000 for married, $18,000 head-of-household, and $12,000 for all other taxpayers, adjusted for inflation;
- An expanded AMT exemption to $109,400 for married and $70,300 for single;
- Many itemized deductions and AGI deductions were suspended or trimmed (more on this later);
- Mortgage debt lowered on new loans;

- Personal exemptions suspended;
- Child tax credit increased;
- New 20% deduction for pass-through income with many limitations;
- Pease itemized deduction limitation suspended;
- ACA shared responsibility payment was lowered to zero for non-compliance with the individual mandate starting in 2019;
- Children's income is no longer subject to taxation at the parent's rate; kids must file tax returns to report earned income, and unearned income is subject to tax using the tax brackets for trusts and estates.

Cap SALT at $10,000 per year. TCJA caps SALT itemized deductions at $10,000 yearly ($5,000 for married filing separately). TCJA allows any combination of state and local income, sales, real estate, or domestic property taxes. SALT may not include foreign real property taxes.

Many business owners deduct home office (HO) expenses, which include real estate taxes, and that allocation is not subject to the $10,000 SALT limit. Here's a tip: To maximize the HO deduction, enter real estate taxes from Schedule A on Form 8829 line 11, and "excess real estate taxes" are not subject to the SALT limitation on line 17.

When you factor in a more substantial standard deduction and how AMT trimmed the state tax deduction for prior years, many individuals may not lose as much of their SALT deduction as they feared. They might have an overall tax cut due to the lower individual tax rates.

About 30 states enacted SALT cap workaround laws (see Chapter 19).

Medical expenses modified. TCJA retained the medical-expense itemized deduction, which is allowed if it exceeds the AGI threshold. In 2017, the AGI threshold was 10% for taxpayers under age 65 and 7.5% for those aged 65 or older. TCJA uses a 7.5% AGI threshold.

Mortgage debt lowered on new loans. As of Dec 15, 2017, new acquisition indebtedness is limited to $750,000 ($375,000 for married taxpayers filing separately), down from $1 million, on a primary residence and second home. Mortgage debt incurred before Dec 15, 2017, is subject to the grandfathered $1 million limit ($500,000 for married taxpayers filing separately). If a taxpayer has a binding written contract to purchase a home before Dec 15, 2017, and to close by Jan 1, 2018, they are grandfathered under the previous limit. Refinancing debt from before Dec 15, 2017, keeps the grandfathered limit, providing the mortgage is not increased.

Per the IRS site, "TCJA suspends the deduction for interest paid on home equity loans and lines of credit unless they are used to buy, build or substantially improve the taxpayer's home that secures the loan." Home equity loans must fit within the overall mortgage limits above.

Enter "excess mortgage interest" on Form 8829, line 16, to deduct home office expenses. The mortgage debt limit only applies to Schedule A itemized deductions.

SUSPENDED DEDUCTIONS

Unreimbursed employee business expenses. TCJA suspends unreimbursed employee business expenses (job expenses) deducted on Form 2106 — there is no Form 2106 for 2018 through 2025. Speak with your employer about implementing an accountable reimbursement plan and "use it or lose it" before year-end.

Tax prep and planning fees. TCJA suspended tax compliance (planning and preparation) fees as itemized deductions. Ask your accountant to break down their invoices into individual vs. business costs because the business portion is allowed as a business expense.

Miscellaneous itemized deductions. TCJA suspended "certain miscellaneous itemized deductions subject to the two-percent floor" in the Joint Explanatory Statement (p. 95-98). Here are the highlights of suspended deductions.

Expenses for the production or collection of income:

- Clerical help and office rent in caring for investments;
- Depreciation on home computers used for investments;
- Fees to collect interest and dividends;
- Indirect miscellaneous deductions from pass-through entities;
- Investment fees and expenses;
- Loss on deposits in an insolvent or bankrupt financial institution;
- Loss on traditional IRAs or Roth IRAs when all amounts have been distributed;
- Trustee's fees for an IRA, if separately billed and paid.

Unreimbursed expenses attributable to the trade or business of being an employee:

- Business bad debt of an employee;
- Business liability insurance premiums;
- Damages paid to a former employer for breach of an employment contract;
- Depreciation on a computer a taxpayer's employer requires him to use;
- Dues to professional societies;
- Educator expenses;
- Home office or part of a taxpayer's home used regularly and exclusively for work;
- Job search expenses in the taxpayer's present occupation;
- Legal fees related to the taxpayer's job;
- Licenses and regulatory fees;
- Malpractice insurance premiums;
- Medical examinations required by an employer.

Occupational taxes:

- Research expenses of a college professor;
- Subscriptions to professional journals and trade magazines related to the taxpayer's work;
- Tools and supplies used in the taxpayer's work;
- Purchase of travel, transportation, meals, entertainment, gifts, and lodging related to the taxpayer's work;
- Union dues and expenses;
- Work clothes and uniforms, if required and not suitable for everyday use;
- Work-related education.

Other miscellaneous itemized deductions subject to the 2% floor include:

- The share of deductible investment expenses from pass-through entities.

Personal casualty and theft losses are suspended. TCJA suspended the itemized deduction of personal casualty and theft loss, except for losses incurred in a federally declared disaster. A taxpayer may apply the loss against the gain if they have a personal casualty gain. If deducting home office expenses, enter "excess casualty losses" on Form 8829, line 29.

Gambling loss limitation modified. TCJA added professional gambling expenses to gambling losses in applying the limit against winnings. Professional gamblers may no longer deduct expenses more than net winnings.

Alimony deduction. TCJA suspended alimony deductions for divorce or separation agreements executed in 2019 and subsequent years, and the recipient does not have taxable income.

Moving expenses. Starting in 2018, TCJA suspended the AGI deduction for moving costs, and employees may no longer exclude moving expense reimbursements, either. One exception: Active-duty military members "who move pursuant to a military order and incident to a permanent change of station."

MORE TCJA CHANGES

Ordinary tax rates reduced. TCJA lowered tax rates on ordinary income for individuals for almost all tax brackets and filing statuses. It decreased the top rate to 37% starting in 2018, from 39.6% in 2017. Investors receive this benefit when short-term capital gains are taxed at ordinary rates.

Filing status equalization. TCJA fixed several inequities in filing status, including the tax brackets, by making single, married filing jointly (MFJ), and married filing separately (MFS) brackets equivalent, except for divergence at the top rate of 37% for single filers, retaining some of the marriage penalty. See the 2021 tax brackets: MFS brackets are precisely half the MFJ brackets throughout all the rates, so MFS filers are not penalized on rates. Filing separately could unlock a QBI deduction.

Repeal of recharacterization for Roth IRA conversions. Suppose a 2017 converted Roth account dropped significantly in value in 2018. In that case, a taxpayer could have reversed the Roth conversion with a "recharacterization" by the tax return's due date, including extensions (Oct 15, 2018). That option is no more; TCJA repealed it starting with 2018 Roth IRA conversions.

Charitable contribution deduction limitation increased. TCJA raised the 50% limitation of AGI for cash contributions to public charities and certain private foundations to 60%. Excess contributions can be carried forward for five years.

TCJA retained charitable contributions as an itemized deduction. But, with the suspension of SALT over the $10,000 cap and certain miscellaneous itemized deductions subject to the 2% floor, many taxpayers are expected not to itemize. Some taxpayers won't feel the deduction effect from making charitable contributions.

Consider a bunching strategy: You can double up on charity one year to itemize and contribute less the next year to use the standard deduction. Another bunching strategy is to set up a charitable trust.

Per TCJA, retirees who must take required minimum distributions by age 70½ (raised to 72 under the SECURE Act) should consider "qualified charitable distributions" (QCD). This move satisfies the RMD rule with the equivalent of an offsetting charitable deduction, allowing you to take the standard deduction rather than itemize.

Expanded use of 529 account funds. TCJA significantly expanded the permitted use of Section 529 education savings account funds. "Qualified higher education expenses" include elementary or secondary public, private, or religious school tuition. (Check with your state.)

Chapter 18

CARES Act

Congress enacted the Coronavirus Aid, Relief, and Economic Security Act (CARES) on March 27, 2020. CARES temporarily affected 2018, 2019, and 2020 taxes by overriding the 2017 Tax Cuts and Jobs Act (TCJA) elements. For example, CARES provided five-year NOL carryback refund claims, whereas TCJA allowed NOL carryforwards. CARES also waived TCJA's excess business loss limitation (EBL). These changes are temporary; TCJA applies again in 2021 through 2025. Recent tax laws extended the EBL limitation to 2028. Trader tax status (TTS) business expenses and Section 475 ordinary losses comprise EBL and an NOL. (See TCJA changes in Chapter 18).

The CARES Act provides tax relief and economic aid to employees, independent contractors, sole proprietors, and other small businesses. However, traders don't fit into usual small-business categories, so there are issues in applying for some CARES aid.

Traders eligible for TTS operating in an S-Corp might be able to receive state and federal unemployment benefits. TTS S-Corps do not qualify for a forgivable loan under the Small Business Administration (SBA) Paycheck Protection Program (PPP) because trading is a "speculative business." TTS traders structured as sole proprietors, partnerships, or S-Corps might be eligible for CARES five-year NOL carrybacks, relaxed retirement plan distributions, and recovery rebates.

A trader's capital gains and Section 475 ordinary income differ from wages, earned income, and self-employment income (SEI) required for many business-related benefits under CARES. TTS sole proprietors report business expenses on Schedule C. Trading gains and losses go on other tax forms, including Schedule D (capital gains and losses) or Form 4797 (Section 475 ordinary gain or loss). In the eyes of government agencies, trading generates investment income derived from the sale of capital assets; it's not a usual small business with revenue.

CARES ALLOWS NOL CARRYBACKS

As discussed in Chapter 17, TCJA repealed two-year NOL carrybacks and only allowed NOL carryforwards limited to 80% of the subsequent year's taxable income starting in tax year 2018. TCJA introduced the "excess business loss" (EBL) limitation, where aggregate business losses over an EBL threshold ($500,000 for married and $250,000 for other taxpayers for 2018) are considered an NOL carryforward.

CARES suspended TCJA's EBL limitation for 2018, 2019, and 2020 and permitted five-year NOL carrybacks for 2018, 2019, and 2020 NOLs.

Business owners could consider amending 2018, 2019, and 2020 tax returns to remove EBL limitations and consider a five-year NOL carryback refund claim. If you haven't elected Section 475 as of year-end 2024, the next opportunity is for 2025, with an election statement due by April 15, 2025.

Businesses had until June 30, 2020, to file a 2018 Form 1045 (quickie refund) for a 2018 NOL carryback. Otherwise, they need Form 1040-X, which allows the IRS more time to process the refund.

TTS traders with Section 475 ordinary losses and those without 475 who have significant NOLs from expenses should consider NOL carrybacks. If Congress changes the rules again, the IRS should respect the refund claim since it was filed based on current law in effect at the time.

RETIREMENT PLAN DISTRIBUTIONS

Taxpayers negatively impacted by COVID-19 could withdraw up to $100,000 from an IRA or qualified retirement plan in 2020 and be exempt from the 10% excise tax on "early withdrawals." The taxpayer can return (rolling over) the funds within three years or pay income taxes on the 2020 distribution over three years. CARES also suspended the required minimum distributions for 2020. (See this May 4, 2020, update on the IRS Website: https://tinyurl.com/coronavirus-tax-qa.)

CHARITABLE DEDUCTIONS

CARES created an above-the-line charitable deduction for 2020 (not to exceed $300). It also modified the AGI limitations on charitable contributions for 2020 to 100% of AGI for individuals (raised from 60% in TCJA).

PARTNERSHIPS AND S-CORPS

The July 15, 2020, virus relief extended deadline did not apply to calendar-year 2019 partnership and S-Corp tax returns and 2020 Section 475 elections for partnerships and S-Corps, all due March 16, 2020. IRS relief guidance mentioned pass-through entities for the July 15 postponement deadline, but that's for a fiscal-year partnership or S-Corp tax return due on or after April 1, 2020.

2020 ESTIMATED TAXES

The Treasury also postponed Q1 and Q2 quarterly estimated tax payments for 2020 until July 15, 2020. (The third and fourth quarters kept their original due dates.)

STATES ALSO POSTPONED THE DEADLINE

All states with a personal income tax extended their April 15 due dates. See the AICPA state filing conformity chart: https://tinyurl.com/conformity-chart.

Check if your state is decoupling from CARES, such as for NOL carrybacks.